THE FATHER IS VERY FOND OF ME

Experiences in the Love of God

To Fergus ~
whose love affair with
the Lord will always give
joy to others. May you always
rejoice in the knowledge that
the Father is very fond of you!

All our love,
Joe, Deen & kids

Christmas 1975

THE FATHER IS VERY FOND OF ME

Experiences in the Love of God

by

Edward J. Farrell

DIMENSION BOOKS
Denville, New Jersey

DEDICATED

*To the Detroit Mission in Recife, Brazil:
Bob, John, Joan, Dorothy, Pat, Ann and
Carol,
To Bill Boteler and Jerry McCrane and all
the Maryknoll priests and sisters in Bolivia
and Peru,
To Claire and the Tertians at the Ursuline
Generalate in Rome,
in gratitude for your hospitality, friendship
and inspiration.*

Published by

DIMENSION BOOKS, INC.
Denville, New Jersey 07834

Copyright © 1975 by Edward J. Farrell

CONTENTS

Foreword   5

I.   Letter from South America
Evangelization   7

II.   The Father, Love or Dread?   30

III.   Pilgrimage to Reconciliation   44

IV.   Prayer in Depth   66

V.   Apostolic Prayer: Praying in
the Midst of Work   107

VI.   Contemplation: Human
Experience of the Love
of God   120

VII.   Poverty   133

VIII.   Celibacy: New Frontier in
Human Sexuality   142

IX.   The Parish Priest: Priest of
the Multitudes   167

X.   Whatever Happened to the
Church?   194

XI.   Letter from Rome: Opening
of the Holy Year Door   209

XII.   Celtic Meditations   221

Postscript Commemoration:
A Sacred Place   232

FOREWORD

In August of 1974 I was doing retreat work in Bolivia and a great Maryknoll priest, Fr. Denny Brown from San Francisco invited me to visit his mission in Montero near Santa Cruz. We spent a delightful evening together and he shared with me much of his rich experience as a missioner. He told me a story, about a priest visiting Ireland, which I will never forget. One evening as the priest walked along the country road he came across an old man also out enjoying the twilight air. They walked and talked together until a sudden rain made them take shelter. When their conversation moved into silence, the old Irishman took out his little prayerbook and began praying half aloud. The priest watched him a long while, then in a quiet whisper said, "You must be very close to God!" The old man smiled very deeply and answered, *"Yes! He is very fond of me!"*

These words have been singing in my mind and heart ever since. *Yes! He is very fond of me!* If I could but believe this truth! I do not have to earn his love; it is gift. All is gift! Perhaps the most profound experience of humility is found in the first moment of love. The first Christian prayer is a "Magnificat," Mary's eucharistic prayer of humble, dancing gratitude for the gift of the Incarnation, the eternal sign of his fondness for us. In South America, I began to learn how poor I was in myself, yet how gifted I was in others, in their experience of Jesus, of the Church. These chapters are explorations in prayer of the gifts he has given to us, of the future to which he calls us, of our ever unfolding experiences of the love of God. TRULY, HE IS VERY FOND OF US.

> He is very fond of the poor.
> He is fond of the Church.
> He is fond of the sinner.
> He is fond of the priest.
> He is very fond of our prayer.

I LETTER FROM SOUTH AMERICA

"Recife." The plane had arrived an hour and a half late. It was already 10:30 P.M. A heavy rain was just letting up. The cabs at the airport entrance were too expensive, so with my baggage in hand we walked out to the highway. The road being under construction, my first step into the semi-darkness was a step into a puddle up to my ankle. The night air was warm and humid and within minutes I was in profuse sweat. Eventually a cab turned up and we headed for the "suburb" of Nova Discoberta (New Discovery) on the northwest rim of the city. We left the cab at the road and began climbing the fairly steep dirt path up the hill. Nova Discoberta is built on parallel hillsides with the road running down the middle. As we climbed up and up, I perspired more and more and began to wonder what I had gotten myself into. Then suddenly we were "home"—an adobe house, with wall to wall cement flooring. No glass, no screen windows, just wooden shutters. No plumbing. No garbage disposal or refuse pickup. This was my introduction to Detroit's mission parish, nine thousand miles from the Cathedral. Two diocesan priests, Bob Singelyn and John Wyskiel and five I.H.M. sisters from Monroe staff the

7

mission. The language is Portuguese. There are sixty thousand people in the parish, all nominally Catholic; about a hundred families participate in the liturgical and community life of the parish.

It took me a long time to be comfortable in the life-style of our diocesan missionaries. To travel in another country a la Hotel is one thing; to plunge into the living situation of the very poor is quite another. I did not realize how conditioned I had become to our high hygienic culture. I never got used to the sight and smell of open garbage dumping, but what bothered me most was the never ending bombardment and invasion of full volume, high amplified radios from four o'clock in the morning until 2:00 A.M. the following morning. I am not sure that they ever went off but in my sleep there seemed to be at least a couple of hours when the noise died down. Next to the absence of silence, what got to me was the absence of privacy, of being able to shut all doors and be alone. There were no doors to shut! And there was no end to people. With the poor one is always crowded. The richer you are the more space you can buy, the more distance you can create, the further you can get from people and the more solitude and silence you can have. From this aspect my experience in the desert was by comparison a luxury! The poor you have always *with* you.

Once I learned to cope with these factors

I began to enter more freely into the life of the missioners. Their life-style seemed to me to come closest to the early Christian communities of the Acts of the Apostles. "These remained faithful to the teaching of the apostles, to the brotherhood, to the breaking of the bread and to the prayers" (Acts 2.42)...."They went as a body to the Temple every day but met in their houses for the breaking of bread; they shared their food gladly and generously; they praised God and were looked up to by everyone. Day by day the Lord added to their community those destined to be saved" (Acts 2.46).

But the richness of the people more than compensates for whatever physical conditions one must endure. You cannot but be humbled by the joy and warmth of these people. Perhaps it was from his experience in Algeria with similar poor that Camus learned that "to protect against a world of unhappiness, you have to create happiness." A Fiesta is celebrated not because there is something to celebrate, but often because of the fact that there is nothing to celebrate! Such is the spirit of the *believing* poor! These are the moments when you can almost believe that you are in a tropical paradise where everyone smiles to you through your open window and a chorus of voices can always be heard in the open theatre of life. Then in an instant you are back to the harshness of barely surviving in the dirt and clutter, the grime and the crumbling. The cry of the poor is the same all over the world, the muted crime against hope itself, the immediate recall, flash back, replay of Taiwan, Mexico, Italy, Detroit!

I shall never forget Dona Rosa's Mass one of my last evenings in Recife. It was Dona Rosa's birthday. She is blind and lives with her blind husband off in the hills on the edge of the parish. It threatened rain but that did not diminish the crowd which gathered in front of the Chapel to walk in the dark to Dona Rosa's home. Some fortunately had flashlights when we left the road to grope our way up the path to her house on the hillside. She had no electricity and needed none, being blind, but for the rest of us there were clusters of three candles well arranged around the crowded living room. There were as many leaning in the windows as had gathered inside. Dona Rosa is a holy woman, the saint of the parish and she has more wisdom than anyone with eyes. She welcomed each one with an embrace knowing each one by voice. You are always comfortable with a holy person because they are all love and can only experience the best in you. What a Mass by candlelight that was! And Dona Rosa with her eyes straight ahead piercing the darkness read the epistle with her fingertips running over her braille scripture. I don't remember her words, my Portuguese was next to nil, but her soul filled the whole room and her spirit lit a birthday candle in each of our hearts. Truly an upper room experience. She had made a cake for us and after tea we wound ourselves back to our own places. It was raining heavily but the rain did not penetrate our clothes, probably dried by the warmth left in us by Dona Rosa!

As I write, so many memories, so many faces come back, like Sr. Joanie. She is the youngest of the sisters and has a beautiful and radiant face with such dancing brown eyes! She could be barely thirty. Her work? A cancer ward! She had no nurses' training so she learned to be an aide and now changes the patients' bandages each day, day after day. I asked her how she could do it, for I knew it would be impossible for me. She said it was impossible for her until she experienced her first patient. As she was about to pass out, the words of Consecration came to her: "This is my body given for you; this is my blood to be shed for you." She does it now with great joy and peace.

Eduardo is an Oblate of St. Francis de Sales from New York. He is a priest-worker in Recife and drives a taxi. I had lunch with him one day. He was returning from celebrating a Mass for the forty-seventh taxi driver to be murdered this year in Recife. This was the last week in July! Life is cheap when people are desperate. Jesus was a carpenter. Eduardo is a taxi driver. The Incarnation-kenosis continues. Christ is with us, there is resurrection everywhere, the resurrection of calling people back to life, telling them the Good News of who they are and how valuable they are before God and before the mystery of my own life. He is with them because I am. They are worth his life, they are worth my life.

I remember Don Helder Camera on a weekend with his lay leaders. He was with them each day, all day. It was so obvious that he was willing to bear the suffering of his people within himself. He had espoused their poverty and simplicity of life. He sat on the episcopal throne as a poor man. "That first day I comprehended Christ the King," powerful because he has no power of this world. "Charity to all" is the breath of his life. He calls the "Abrahamic minorities" to celebrate each day as a new holy day and to rejoice in the freedom to move with the Spirit, to make a mistake. I enjoyed his fourfold description of leadership: Leadership is like a *tractor*: hooks up and pulls, gets a lot of work done; like a *cat*: who wants to get into the house; you put him out one door and he comes in by back window; like a *preacher*: who is always explaining, everything is a word; like a *brother*: who walks where you are, learns your pace. Brother—that is what Don Helder is, oldest brother who suffers and worries most for the family. Last year his young priest secretary was kidnapped and murdered in cold blood, his body dumped alongside the Catholic university as a threat to him and to his people.

Few men appear at the "evangelization groups" in the parish because they cannot afford to "disappear" as had happened to several men of the parish the previous year. I talked to one of the men who "disappeared"—held, threatened and tortured, he would say little because of danger to his family. But the stories of repression and persecution are no exaggeration. I wonder which is the Church of Silence? The Church Silenced under martial law or the Church in free countries, silent about the injustice and repression in the rest of the world. "If only one man in the world is not free, no one of us is free." We are still far from being Catholic, from being so intimately united that if one weeps, the other will taste the salt! The Church of the twentieth century needs not more theologians but more confessors. Don Helder and so many of his people are our confessors. I caught a final glimpse and had a warm embrace from Don Helder at the airport as he carried someone else's luggage to the gate.

As my plane lifted above Recife I experienced a deep gratitude for the new experience of Nazareth and a discovery of my unknown brothers and sisters whom my Father had revealed to me. I re-treasured the thought of a Dutch priest recently returned from a pilgrimage to Our Lady of Guadalupe. Wherever Our Lady has appeared in the last four centuries, it has been to the poor and to the theologically unsophisticated. She continues to call the Church back to her deepest roots. "The poor you will have always with you" which for me has become a beatitude; the truth you will have always with you. Recife is Christ crucified and risen. I prayed "take me into your heart, which loves, creates so extravagantly and abundantly, with all these your children, your sparks of life, your body, your presence: being—life—love—friendship: faith, hope, love—where two or three are gathered—two pieces of flint producing a spark—a candle—a flame. Taking in the life of another, entering into more life, more love. More life through struggle and overcoming." There is an intensity of life and love necessary to overcome destitution, injustice and victimization. Maximum depth and spiritual resources are demanded. When there is nothing outside, exterior, everything has to be created inside, inwardly. To drink of the inner well, inner heart; there is nothing to give but faith, hope and love: joy, peace, friendship.

Recife was the eleventh station for me, the stripping of all the garments of my culture, losing of so many of my illusions. It was an experience of radical inner poverty. My flesh screamed "I can't do it"—dressing terminally ill cancer patients, living in garbage, dampness, dirt and stench with no achievement, completion, fulfillment possible. The total silence of God!, the unstoppable internal and external bleeding of one's people, the complete daily dependence on the Spirit of Jesus. This day our daily bread. Unless you die, you cannot bear fruit—the inner kinds of dying; the inner kinds of life. Mary with the poor. Being evangelized by the poor, being Gospelled! "Without me you can do nothing!" Laying down one's life daily not on my own terms but on someone else's. "This is my body given for you; this is my blood shed for you." Reduced to one's knees. I live now not I! So much *I* to my life, so little *him*. I will gladly spend and be spent for your sakes. Intense love for him, for his body, these alone can overcome the cultural shocks. Your Kingdom come in me! *Sell* all that you have, *give* it to the poor and *come* follow me. New reading of the Gospel! New need for stripping. New stations of the Cross. No private life; life always in the open. To love like that, to die like that. To do always what Jesus would do!

Achacachi, Desaquadero, Yunguyo, Pomato, Juli, Illave, Acora, Mocachi, Chucuito, Puno, Juliaca—a litany of strange sounding names, the towns along the east and west shores of Lake Titicaca, the common border of Boliva and Peru. In the fifteenth and sixteenth century around this lake, the highest on earth—13,500 ft.—the Spanish Dominican and Jesuit missionaries established the "Church." Every thirty miles, a day's walking, they built what we would call monumental basilicas, most of which have survived structurally intact through four centuries. The Franciscan missions of the California coast would be a distant echo of this achievement. What faith and genius created these symbols of worship! The magnificence and grandeur of the Andes mountains must have fired in them a heroic expansiveness and a sense of monumental greatness which attempted then to rival the power and beauty of nature around them. This would be the setting for my month of retreats with the Maryknoll missioners of Bolivia and Peru. Recife had prepared me well. I was to be awed and humbled as much by these men as I was by the Andes crusted with their winter snows. These were men shaped and formed by near inaccessible mountains which barely granted them survival. These men towered over me as much as did the mountains. These men had gathered together to pray, to relocate themselves with Christ. They had come not for a day or two but for a full week. I asked each of them to share with each other what they were seeking. "To move from servant to friend. To rest and listen to Christ. Deeper motivation for consistent prayer life. Deeper prayer life for my people. Not free enough for him. Restless, lying to myself. Recognize Spirit working in me. Community. No time to pray. Do anything but pray. I need to experience the conviction and faith of my brother priests! What more is there to prayer? To know where I am. To put myself in touch with God. Dominated by the situation. Want to see where my priesthood is now and will be in the future. Light for what he wants from me from here on. I experience not only my need but my emptiness. Lost in projects. Who, what, where, perspective. . . .Prayer as something. . . .Girl twenty-four years old who will die of cancer before I return. . . .Fill tank. . . .My life is too much in the screw or be screwed situation. Relation with Christ. I need a good block of time. Rest and personal integration. Prayer of the heart. Can't we begin again. Intimate search for God. Why do I stay? I pray two and a half hours a day. How do I go deeper?"

These are the voices of honest-to-God men, lean men who waste no words and have no time to waste. Our prayer was "Father, out of your infinite glory, give us the power through your Spirit for our hidden priesthood to grow strong, so that Christ may live in our hearts" (Ephesians 3.16) We began on the eve of the Transfiguration and it seemed that it was he, himself, who took us up to the mountain to pray. The transfiguration took place only once in the lifetime of the apostles and they had to live out of it the rest of their lives. We know that the Eucharist is our daily transfiguration which makes us his transfiguration, the resurrection going on in the life of his people. "Lord help our unbelief! Strengthen our power to love, to hope, to believe. Jesus in us enable us to speak, to be to the

Father, to become sons!" there is no one to whom we can be closer than to Father, Son, and Spirit. Faith, hope, and love is the same experience under different facets and faucets of the divine presence and spark within us. Contemplation is not in the breadth of the day but in the depth of the moment. The depth of our need is the experience of our nothingness. Yet Jesus is our hidden self—our unknown self who creates the unknown soldier, the unknown saint. Holiness is usually unexperienced, love is ordinarily unfelt, un-understood. There is an Adam within us, but also an Abraham, a Moses, a Jesus! His hand is upon us, we experience more and more the Father in us, the Breath of his Love. I am growing into his life in me, I am becoming more and more son. The Father tells me again and again: "all things are yours, you are Christ's and Christ is mine." He calls me by name; "Edward my son! I forbid you to be afraid. Be at peace. I am with you." He shares his name with me; everyone calls me father. I wonder what kind of a father I would be? What kind of a father would I want to be? What kind of a father am I? He invites me to contemplative depth, to be my Father's son, to be Jesus' brother. I am not sure if I want to accept all my thoughts and ideas; I push them away. I want to pray but I cannot pray. I am growing into something, but "I do not know what I am to become." So I pray from where I am, with my people, with my brothers. Without you I can do nothing.

To be son of the Father is to be in union with him as much as with myself everywhere and at every moment. Do with me what you will; whatever you do I thank you—people, health, weather. Do not be afraid. I want to be open to all that happens, discerning how each experience affects me, being a little child before everything which comes to be. What new gifts does his love bring to me today? Being in the Father's presence, rejoicing, praying always, continual thanksgiving for his goodness—in this spirit how easy it is to sing Psalm 131, my favorite:

> Yahweh, my heart has no lofty ambitions,
>   my eyes do not look too high.
> I am not concerned with great affairs or
>   marvels beyond my scope.
> Enough for me to keep my soul tranquil and
>   quiet like a child in its Mother's arms,
>   as content as a child that has been weaned.

But more often the missioner must pray Hebrews 12:13—"All of these died in faith, receiving any of the things that had been promised, but they saw them in the far distance and welcomed them, recognizing that they were only strangers and nomads on earth."

In 1574 along the shore of a certain section of Lake Titicaca there were three priests, all of them foreigners. In 1974, four hundred years later, in the same area there are three priests, still all of them foreign. In the Maryknoll seminary at Juli over a period of twenty years there have been eight hundred seminarians; only five of them have ever been ordained.

"The harvest is rich but the laborers are few, so ask the Lord of the harvest to send laborers to his vineyard" (Luke *10*.3). Many non-missionary communities of men and women and many diocesan priests responded to the prayer and call of Pius XII in the fifties to send a tenth of their personnel to South America. Aside from our diocesan mission in Recife, I met diocesan priests from St. Louis, Kansas City, New York, Boston, Buffalo, etc. I believe that there are over two hundred diocesan priests from more than forty dioceses working in South America today in diocesan missions or as associates of Maryknoll. Whatever they may accomplish in South America, will be secondary, I believe, to the great work which lies ahead of them back in the States. Here they must become a leaven and ferment to begin and continue evangelization among our own people enkindling in us a real depth in being Catholic and universal brothers and sisters.

As the days went on I asked the men why they had become missioners. Since it is difficult to speak of that which lies deep within the heart their answers ranged from "it's like playing the horses. . .it's in your blood" to "the mission spirit is intrinsic to every Christian." Something or someone compelled them to go forth. "It's a calling that is constant, you know it is your place, like a nail knows a magnet." It's a vocation within a vocation, a call within a call. Someone else described it as a "charism of universal love"—a commitment in faith to meet with people with a great deal of friendship, to be open to a stranger with love and compassion. The common denominator seemed to be that they were men who had left their own home to preach the Gospel or rather to *be* the Gospel in an area which was not their own from birth. Theirs is a special form of poverty that of becoming a "universal brother" in imitation of the emptying out of Jesus. It is not an extended form of tourism nor is it a doing of the Peace Corps stint. A man, without ever ceasing to be what he is, enters and becomes part of a different culture at the present moment in a given place. He is to witness with his life to a different people the relativity of human convictions in the face of the unique and absolute meaning of revelation. He will never be more than an adopted son. He will always be behind; you cannot catch up on a lifetime. To learn a language is to relinquish one's own world of thoughts and associations and expressions as the standard measure of fully developed thought. A spiritual ascesis and kenosis is demanded. One must be willing literally to die and be reborn in the adopted culture. One must be re-created in the Spirit.

The missionary presence is ever strange. It is an expression of the weakness of Christ, the weakness of the priest. It is ever a replay of the prologue of John's Gospel, "and the world did not know him. He came to his own and his own people did not accept him. But to all who did accept him, he gave power to become children of God" (John 1:10).

The questions are ever new, the answers are few. Dead is the question: "Whose ball park are we going to play in—their culture or ours?" Everyone is more than aware of the danger of spiritual imperialism, of the problems with ourselves, of projecting our own needs on the people. The norm is the Acts of the Apostles, the poverty of the radical life even though "you know that if you try to go native you could be dead in a month." So one commits himself to be a piling, to be driven into the ground and disappear for some future missioner to build upon, to be buried there like seeds in a desert waiting for the promised rain. It is hard to look forward to the fourth or fifth generation, to work from below rather than from above. You cannot preach to the poor. You have to be there in the simple presence of love and service under a covenant of fidelity until death. "One grows in silence with men and with God—to learn the full meaning of one, we must practice the other and deepen it."

What is the value of one person? The silence and hiddenness of a person is as mysterious and secret as God's. Every person is an invitation to go deeper, to enter in reverence to the hidden presence of God. The contemplation and adoration of another person is inexhaustible, demanding ever greater depth of seer and listener. One must wait for the curtain between people to be drawn back before one approaches the inner door to the heart, the inner window of the soul. One must "hold" at a distance until the work of presence, listening, response has its cumulative effect in the interiorization of the other. This mutual indwelling becomes a mutual creativity, discovering and releasing the power of the Spirit and the resurrection. In the "in *me*ing you and the in *you*ing me, incorporation, ingrafting of his Body takes place. The visitation of Mary and Elizabeth is the paradigm of all evangelization. "She went into Zechariah's house and greeted Elizabeth. Now as soon as Elizabeth heard Mary's greeting, the child leapt in her womb and Elizabeth was filled with the Holy Spirit" (Luke *1*:41).

The mystery of Evangelization; of being the Good News, of going and making disciples of all nations! How little I understood of that word until my exposure to South America. I was compelled to reread Vatican II's Document "Ad Gentes." What follows is my digest of that document: The numbers are the particular paragraphs: The

Church is the universal sacrament of salvation. Jesus was missioned by the Father.
The Incarnation was the first mission. As
the Holy Spirit overshadowed Mary to
bring forth Christ, so "Christ was impelled
to the work of his ministry when the same
Holy Spirit descended on him at prayer (4)
(Luke *3:*22; *4:*1, Acts *10:* 38). She undertakes
this activity in obedience to Christ's command and in response to the grace and love
of the Holy Spirit by the example of her
life and teaching. . . .She leads them to the
faith, freedom and *peace* of *Christ.* (5) The
truth and grace found among the nations is
a sort of secret presence of God. "Enlarge
the space for your tent, spread out your
tent cloths unsparingly" (Isaiah *54:*2) (9). The
same way Christ bound himself by the
cultural and social conditions of the persons with whom he dwelt. (10) Gladly and
reverently laying bare the seeds of the
Word which lie hidden in the national and
religious traditions. (11)

How Christian religious life may be able
to assimilate the ascetic and contemplative
traditions whose seeds were sometimes
already planted by God in ancient cultures
prior to the teaching of the gospel. . .For
the contemplative life belongs to the fullness of the Church's presence and should
be established everywhere. (18)

This was very powerfully brought home
to me by Fr. Innocentia Salazar, a Mary-
knoller from Texas. He has worked for ten
years among the Aymara Indians of the

Altiplano of Peru. He told me that our difficulty lies in fact that we do not know *how* to know. He graciously shared with me his journal, writings and slides of his work among the Indians. I hope he will publish them soon. What follows are excerpts from his writings: "The sacred is not an absolute value but relative to the situation. Group events are rites of intensification. These restore the equilibrium where change in social interaction occur. Rites are good for understanding analysis of interaction. Religious rites re-establish whatever unbalance confronts people e.g. matrimony, separation from home, beginning of a new life, inauguration of a new house." They project so much of their hopes into a rite that it does become true. Symbol-making is creating those events and participating in them in such a way that we and others draw a sense of direction in life.

Then Salazar asks, "Unless our religion, our talking with God represents that of the Pagos and Yatiris (local priests) what good are we doing?". . . .We should write down our feelings as we pray or study or read Scripture because those feelings are leads to what the Lord is telling us. The Lord is present in Scripture and the way he moves us will be registered in our feelings. It should be done in groups as much as possible. As a result, when we perform rites, the thing that will come across is not that we are merely ritual men but rather that we are men of prayer, men of God.

Prayer is a way to talk to God, to praise him, to be in touch with him, to love him and feel his love.

"We need a contemplative group and a sanctuary where people may go and talk with God. It could be called "The Place of the Loving Father—Come and talk with him." The Mass should be a spiritual confrontation and consultation whose words of wisdom would be exchanged. We must thrash out our role as ritual men; thrash out our own spirituality and not be afraid to express our consistency or inconsistency whatever the case may be." (11 Oct. 1971)

These souls are marked by a special vocation. . . .They are set apart for the special work to which they have been called (Ad Gentes) (23). Abounding joy in the depths of poverty (2 Corinthians *8*:2, nor neglect the grace of God that is in them, be renewed day by day in Spirit and in mind (1 Timothy *4:*14; Ephesians *4:*23; 2 Corinthians *4*:16) (24).

Universality of the Church and diversity of the world's nations (26). The experience of Paul is echoed down to our day: "One night Paul had a vision: A Macedonian appeared and appealed to him in these words, 'Come across to Macedonia and *help* us'. Once he had seen this vision, he *lost no time* in arranging a passage to Macedonia *convinced that God had called us to bring them the Good News*" (Acts

16.9). And thus the Gospel passed into Europe and into our lives!

In some other reading I came across an address of Pope Paul's to Peasants at Bogata during the Eucharistic Congress of 1968. "You are a sign, you are an image, you are a mystery of the presence of Christ. The sacrament of the Eucharist offers us his hidden presence, living and real. But you too are a sacrament i.e. a sacred image of the Lord among us, as it were a revealing, unconcealed reflection of his human and divine countenance. . . .and all the Church's tradition recognizes in the poor the sacrament of Christ—a mystical correspondence with the Eucharist."

The retreats finished, I am on my way to Detroit. I can see the incredible peaks of the Andes piercing the clouds at 28,000 feet! I wonder at all I have seen and heard. I experience a deep gratitude for the past seven weeks. I have a need to identify in some way with those missionaries and their people. I decide to give up cocktails and beer. It is not a great gesture but it will be a continuing reminder of my brothers and sisters. I open my New Testament and the first words I read are: "I have sent you to reap a harvest for which you have never laboured; other men have worked hard and you have reaped the result of their labors." Wow! I alone knew how radically true those words were. Father, let me never forget!

The reality of evangelization and development was seared into me. The world Church, the whole Church is forever in need of evangelization. I feel that Detroit is in need of as much evangelization as is Recife or Achacachi. In fact, it is obvious that not a little of the problem of South America is the evangelization of our own economic policies, politics and international presence. Like the prophet of old, Habakkuk, I felt as if I had been lifted up by the hair of my head and deposited in another country in order to see myself.

"Wealth is indeed a treacherous thing
Haughty and unable to rest is he
who is greedy as Sheol,
who is like death, insatiable,
who assembles all the nations for his own ends,
collects all the people to his own advantage."
(Habakkuk 2:5).

The mass of mankind seems untouched by the Spirit, by love. The cumulative condition of sin continues unredeemed. One can be easily lost in the immensity of visible evil, indifference, apathy. Yet there is an immense struggle for good, for justice, for peace. There is a never diminishing number of men and women who hear the Abrahamic-Christ call: "Leave your country, your family and your father's house, for the land that I will show you " (Genesis 12:1).

"With so many witnesses in a great cloud on every side of us, we too, then should throw off everything that hinders us, especially the sin that clings to us, and keep running steadily in the race that we have started. Let us not lose sight of Jesus, who leads us in our faith and brings it to perfection: for the sake of the joy that was still in the future, he endured the cross. . . . make sure that you never refuse to listen when he speaks. The people who refused to listen to the warning from a voice on earth could not escape their punishment, and now shall we escape if we turn away from a voice that warns us from heaven? That time, his voice made the earth shake, but now he has given us promise: I shall make the earth shake once more and not only the earth but heaven as well. The words once more show that since the things being shaken are created things, they are going to be changed so that the unshakeable things will be left. We have been given possession of an unshakeable kingdom. Let us therefore hold on to the grace that we have been given and use it to worship God in the way that he finds acceptable, in reverence and fear. For our God is a consuming fire" (Hebrews 12).

II THE FATHER: LOVE OR DREAD?

The Father himself loves you (John *16*,27).

. . .and my Father will love him, and we shall come to him and make our home with him (John *14*,23).

Anyone who loves me will be loved by my Father and I shall love him and show myself to him (John *14*,21).

The Father sent his Son as savior of the world (1 John *4*,14).

. . .loved the world so much that he gave his only Son (John *3*,16).

. . .the Father of our Lord Jesus Christ who has blessed us with all the spiritual blessings of heaven in Christ. Before the world was made he chose us, chose us in Christ, to be holy and spotless and to live through love in his presence (Ephesians *1*,3).

Think of the love that the Father has lavished on us by letting us be called God's children; and that is what we are (1 John *3*,1).

. . .has sent the spirit of his Son into our hearts: the Spirit that cries 'Abba, Father ' (Galatians *4*,6).

It is my Father who gives you the bread from heaven (John *6*,32).

Your Father who sees all that is done in secret will reward you (Matthew 6,4).

Your Father knows what you need before you ask him (Matthew 6,8).

The Father of our Lord Jesus Christ, a gentle Father and the God of all consolation, who comforts us in all our sorrows (1 Corinthians 1,3).

I bless you, Father, Lord of heaven and of earth, for hiding these things from the learned and clever and revealing them to mere children (Matthew 11,25).

Look at the birds in the sky. They do not sow or reap or gather into barns; yet your heavenly Father feeds them. Are you not worth much more than they are? (Matthew 6,26).

No one can come to me unless he is drawn by the Father who sent me (John 6,44).

No one knows the Son except the Father, just as no one knows the Father except the Son and those to whom the Son chooses to reveal him (Matthew 11,27).

There is no need to be afraid, little flock, for it has pleased your Father to give you the kingdom (Luke 12,32).

So you should pray like this: Our Father. . . (Matthew 6,9).

"Our Father. . .thy will be done,"—the daily prayer of all Christians, the first prayer learned, the last to be let go of—or so I thought until I began to give work-shops on prayer. There is no illusion easier nor is there one more dangerous than the illusion of prayer—"praying with the lips but their hearts are far from him." I ask people to listen to their own prayer, to pray the "Our Father" in a different translation, to sound out the words, to sound out with what depth they pray the words, "Thy will be done." I tell them to put their prayer into the first person singular, "Father, I abandon myself into your hands," (Luke *23*,46; Psalm *31*,5), Christ's prayer on the cross. I have been astonished over and again how few people, priests, sisters, laity, dare to pray, "I abandon myself into your hands." It is easy to say for the ten-thousandth time "thy will be done" in the sense "que sera sera"—what can I do about it anyway. But to pray, "I abandon myself,"—in no way! What immediately surfaces is a deep *dread*, a radical fear, a basic preconscious convic-tion that one cannot trust God. If you do trust God, the worst will happen to you as it did to Job and to the prophets. You will be stricken with cancer of the brain or some suffering which will be utterly impos-sible for you to bear. This all pervasive *dread* of God is more than a misconceived Yahweh of the Hebrew Scriptures. It is a regression to the pagan gods who were a projection of the dark half of man's uncon-scious and his experience of finiteness and powerlessness. Such is my experience of today's Christian, not the anonymous or fringe variety, but that Christian who most hungers and thirsts for him.

There is in all of us an unresolved dread of God, a dread mixed with anger, resentment. The Psalms reflect this very well and to pray them can be a help in accepting our own repressed violent feelings toward God. But basically and fundamentally this dread of God indicates that the Word of Jesus, the Good News, has not penetrated into, has not taken root in our heart of hearts. Jesus' and the Spirit's first and ultimate Word to us is *Abba*, the Father's love for us. The Word has been heard, received and we believe but with so little faith that "the birds come and eat it up, or the sun scorches and not having any roots, it withers away, or the thorns grow up and choke it."

The work of prayer, its blood, sweat and tears, is to take the word of the mind into the heart and spirit until there is within us an underground nuclear explosion and we "know" the Father and experience the freedom of the children of God which casts out all fear. "In love there can be no fear, but fear is driven out by perfect love: because to fear is to expect punishment and anyone who is afraid is still imperfect in love " (1 John 4:18). Where does one begin to understand the mystery of Jesus revealing God to us as "Father?" Revelation reveals not only God to man but also reveals man and his experience to himself.

Because God is Father, a whole depth of meaning is opened to the human experience of fathering and being fathered. Perhaps our difficulty in responding to God as Father springs from our failure to reflect on our own human experience of fatherhood.

"Father," "Daddy," (Abba), is more than a word; it is an identity, involving a history and a destiny. It is the word which is usually expressed first in our vocabulary and language and since it communicates such a deep experiential relationship, it is one of the last to be understood. "Father" is a word which stands apart from all other words, stands in a class all by itself. Words should be of different sizes and shapes and include a variety in type and line. Significance and depth should have its proportion. "Father" should be three inches high, just a little smaller than "God." "God" is the name which man gave to God; "Father" is what he told man to call him. "Father" is a word which cries out volumes, volumes which cannot be written. We have an example of this mystery in the prisoners of war who came home to six or seven-year-old sons who had to be taught to say, "Father," "Daddy."

The father names his son in a special way with a word; the son names his father in an even more unique way, with his life. The father is born through the son no less than the son is born through the father.

Father: Love or Dread?

Eternal one, to me yourself you showed.
I love you dearly as a dearest son,
who, while a child, forsook me long ago,
for destiny had called him to a throne
before whose state all lands like vales lie low.
I'm left behind like some old greybeard now
who understands his grown-up son no more
and can but little of those new things know
which draw his offspring's will
    with wheedling power.
Sometimes my spirit for your
    deep luck quails,
which borne on many a strange vessel sails.
Sometimes I wish you back to me, back here
into this dark, where you once nurtured were.
Sometimes I'm scared for fear your life
    has ceased,
when in Time's maze I wander hopelessly.
I read of you then: the evangelist
writes everywhere of your eternity.

I am the father; yet the son is more,
is all the father ever was; and one
the father ne'er became, within the son
is taking form and greatly comes to be;
he is the future, the return is he,
he is the womb, he is the sea. . .

Rainer Maria Rilke

A child knows his mother from living within her. The father is the first stranger a child comes to know and to love. "Daddy!" What power there is in a word when it represents half the total vocabulary of the child! How long it takes for a son to come to know his father! It takes half a lifetime to grow into even a dim awareness of what it is to owe one's life, existence and personality to another. One has himself to grow to the age of fathering to even begin to understand what it means to be born of this man, to grow up into this man, to have a father, to be fathered! One never catches up to his own father. The mystery of all that one carries within himself! A human father can actualize only a small fragment of what is within. Ten sons cannot express all the possibilities carried in one father. So, until the end of time will we live out all the possibilities, all the potentialities of Adam, Abraham, Christ.

Often I have asked myself, "What is this experience of being son, my father's son? Am I my father's son? What kind of a son am I?" The Irish have an expression, "I know you out of your father." I wonder what they see that I do not see. What do I recognize of my father in me? What does he recognize of himself in me? How often a son realizes a father's love for him after it is too late to share his realization with him. How rare it is for a father to know his son's love for him. The immense gap in human relationships! The incompleteness of family bonds! How rarely the distance of father and son converge and disappear in the equality of friendship! One envies the Son and his Father. Perhaps the revelation of this mystery is that promise and hope which he alone can keep—the Father drawing every father into his fullness of Fatherhood; the Son drawing every son into the fullness of sonship!

Father: Love or Dread?

My father was 35 when I was born. I was
34 when he died. Death opens a depth-
perception which cannot be released in life.
Something is torn out of the heart. It is like
a huge oak being torn from a small field.
The oak appears to take up a little corner
but its roots fill the whole field. Yet in that
very instant, into that void and emptiness
came a communion which cannot be experienced in life. The world and the life to
come were no longer at a distance. They
had broken as a tidal-wave into my life, the
veil was rent from top to bottom, because
now he who was the source of my life was
"there" and, therefore, I was "there" or
"it" was "here." I remember my words to
myself: "Now you understand, my father
who is in heaven. You who gave me life
have breathed forth your life. Today I feel
that I am more yours than ever before,
because I am what is left of you. You are
to be with me always. Now I am your life,
your heartbeat. I feel the strength of your
presence. Where you are, so much of
myself is present. You are my anchor with
our Father. Where I am, so much of
yourself is present. What you have given to
me, done in me, what you have earned for
me will take my lifetime to unfold. Now I
share with you all the things I was unable
to share with you in life. We never expressed our love for one another enough;
perhaps it was not necessary. Now we live
together in him. Continue your fathering
in me."

Our Father who is in heaven. Slowly a new level of prayer began within me. I became more sensitive to the way in which Jesus spoke to his Father and about his Father, and one of the first Scriptural passages to take on new meaning for me was John 5,17: "My Father goes on working and so do I." Somehow I had imagined that the Father was in retirement and that the Son had taken over the business. Next came the words, "I am never alone, the Father is always with me " (John *8*,16). What a consolation! There can be no loneliness, no solitude with Christ. Then I found the oft-repeated refrain, "I do nothing of myself " (John *8*,28). Slowly I gathered the mosaic of Jesus' words about his Father in relationship to himself:

The Son can do nothing by himself; he can only do what he sees the Father doing. And whatever the Father does the Son does too (John *8*,5,19).

I do nothing of myself: what the Father has taught me is what I preach; he who sent me is with me, and has not left me to myself for I always do what pleases him (John *8*,28).

For what I have spoken does not come from myself; no, what I was to say, what I had to speak, was commanded by the Father who sent me, and I know that his commands mean eternal life, and therefore what the Father has told me is what I speak (John *12*,49).

Do you not believe that I am in the Father and the Father is in me? The words I say to you I do not speak as from myself: it is the Father, living in me who is doing this work (John *14*,10).

My food is to do the will of the one who sent me and to complete his work (John *4*,34).

As I myself draw life from the Father.

They will never be lost and no one will ever steal them from me (John *10*,28).

I can do nothing by myself (John *5*,30).

I must carry out the work of the one who sent me (John *9*,4).

The Father loves the Son and has entrusted everything to him (John *3*,35).

For the Father loves the Son and shows him everything he does himself (John *5*,20).

The Father loves me, because I lay down my life in order to take it up again (John *10*,17).

What I, for my part, speak of is what I have seen with my Father (John *8*,38).

The Father himself loves you (John *16*,27).

That the love with which you loved me may be in them (John *17*,26).

A life "in fellowship with the Father and with his Son " (1 John*1*,3).

The whole of my Fatherly love is poured out on my Son and I shall have to find you in him in order to extend to you too, become one with my Son.

Jesus draws us to himself to lead us to the Father.

I ascend to my Father and to your Father (John *20*,17).

For by him we have access both in one Spirit to the Father (Ephesians *2*,18).

The greatest work of the Son was to bring us to knowledge of the Father. S. Hilary.

Whoever shall do the will of my Father who is in heaven, he is my brother, and sister and mother (Matthew *12*,46).

And whatsoever you shall ask the Father in my name that I do, that the Father may be glorified in the Son (John *14*,13).

I love the Father (John *14*,31).

Jesus never did his own "thing." He did only his Father's "thing." He did his Father so totally and completely that to imitate Jesus is to imitate the Father; to identify with Jesus is to identify with the Father. "To have seen me is to have seen the Father, so how can you say, 'Let us see the Father?' Do you not believe that I am in the Father and the Father is in me?" The tension between prayer and ministry is not found in Jesus, because as he says, "I do nothing of myself." His prayer leads him to ministry, to do what he sees the Father doing, and his ministry always returns him in thanksgiving to the Father "as I myself draw life from the Father" (Job 6,57). Jesus is the perfect mirror, the fullest splendor, the radiant glory of the Father. Jesus' work was to manifest the Father to us, to make us his gift to the Father. We are destined to grow into sonship the whole of our lives, recognizing ever more deeply his fathering of us, knowing him because we grow more and more into his life as he pours more and more of his Spirit into us.

Jesus gives us the Father—there was nothing greater for him to give. Jesus shows us the way to the Father. He is the Way. "To all who did accept him, he gave power to become sons of God." . . .God sent his son. . .to enable us to be adopted as sons. The proof that you are sons is that God has sent the Spirit of his Son into our hearts; the Spirit that cries 'Abba,' Father, and it is this that makes you a son, you are not a slave anymore; and if God has made you son, then he has made you heir, (Galatians 4,4). This is our true identity not only by faith but in the depths of our being. "The Spirit himself gives testimony to our spirit that we are sons of God" (Romans 8,16). Whoever are led by the Spirit of God, they are sons of God, "being freed to enjoy the same freedom and glory as the children of God" (Romans 8,21). "My dear people, we are already the children of God but what we are to be in the future has not yet been revealed; all we know is that when it is revealed, we shall be like him because we shall see him as he really is" (1 John 3,2).

"They are the ones he chose specially long ago and intended to become true images of his Son, so that his Son might be the *eldest of many brothers*" (Romans 8,29).

"No one has ever seen God; it is the only Son, who is nearest to the Father's heart, who has made him known" (1 John 1,18). This was the great redemptive work of Christ—to give us his Father. "I call you friends because I have made known to you everything I have learned from my Father" (John 15,15). The "Our Father" of the synoptic Gospels is actually the prayer of Jesus which he gave to his disciples. It is the seventeenth chapter of John's Gospel which gives us Jesus' prayer to his Father. What a gift—to be able to listen to Jesus' conversation with and prayer to his Father! "All that I have is yours and all you have is mine". . .May they all be one. Father may they be one in us as you are in me and I am in you". . . .that they may be one as we are one. With me in them and you in me". . . I have made your name known to them and will continue to make it known, so that the love with which you loved me may be in them and so that I may be in them."

High in the Andes Mountains of Bolivia at Tiahuanaco near the Capital La Paz, there lie the oldest Indian ruins in South America. There is a statue to a god whose name even the Indians have forgotten. But every representation of this god shows him weeping. I had forgotten that experience until several months later when I celebrated the Eucharist for a group of families who had lost a child either through sickness, accident or violence. The Eucharist took on a special depth because each of these parents experienced so totally the offering of the sacrifice of their own child. And I could not help but experience the tears of the Father with them, and for the first time became aware of the tears which the Father must have wept at the death of his own son. Jesus' tears over the city, for the widow of Naim, for Lazarus, were tears which also came from his Father's heart. What must be the depth of the Father's sorrow, his pain! "The Father and I are one." The crucifixion must have pierced the Father as much as the Son! "Blessed be the God and Father of our Lord Jesus Christ, a gentle Father and the God of all consolation, who comforts us in all our sorrows, so that we can offer others, in their sorrows, the consolation that we have received from God ourselves!" (2 Corinthians *1*,3).

"The Father is love. The Father's love for us was revealed when the Father sent into the world his only Son so that we could have life through him, this is the love I mean: not our love for the Father but the Father's love for us when he sent his Son to be the sacrifice that takes our sins away.

My dear people, since the Father has loved us so much we too should love one another. No one has ever seen the Father; but as long as we love one another, the Father will live in us and his love will be complete in us (1 Job *4*,7).

III PILGRIMAGE TO RECONCILIATION

The word reconciliation is a strange word to most of us—those six syllable vocabulary words do not really charge us, do not really evoke too much from us. Nevertheless reconciliation has become a master theme even though it remains strange to us. The call to prayer is but the first step, the second step is the being sent, being sent as reconciler to make visible the mystery of Christ's presence within. I've come to think of reconciliation as a visible manifestation of the reality of prayer—his presence in us. Let us try to investigate and explore the mystery of Christ as reconciler and the Christian as the one sent to create the presence of Christ among men.

"From now on therefore, we do not judge anyone by the standards of the flesh. Even if we did once know Christ in the flesh that is not how we know him now and for anyone who is in Christ, there is a new creation. The old creation is gone and now the new one is here. It is all God's work." It was God who reconciled us to himself through Christ and gave us the work of handing on this reconciliation. In other words, God in Christ was reconciling the world to himself, not holding men's faults against them. And he has entrusted to us the news that men are reconciled. So we, you and I, are ambassadors for Christ. "It is as though God were appealing through us the appeal that we make in Christ's name, to be reconciled to God. For our sake, God made the one into sin so that in him we might become the goodness of God. As his fellow workers, we beg you once again not to neglect the grace of God that you have received for he says, 'At the favorable time I have listened to you. On the day of Salvation, I came to your help. Now is the favorable time; this is the day of salvation.' " We are ambassadors for Christ; we are his fellow workers.

To what degree can I believe that I am his ambassador, his presence, hold his power? What does it mean to reconcile, to establish bonds, to establish kinship, to establish friendship? What was in Christ in that moment of his human consciousness when he became fully aware of his mission, that he existed for all men? That all mankind, every man, every woman, was to be drawn into himself? And what does it mean for us today to bear the name Christian? The Christian mystery is a constant call to listen, to come, and to go. And prayer is our experience of listening to his word which is always a new word. Again and again we will find a new way, a new prism to see—to see what he is doing, to see what his spirit is saying to us. But we know from experience that we do not do anything we do not have to do, and today we are being pushed as never before. We are in a tremendous evolutionary development, something like a quantum leap. We did not ask to be here, but we are here; and we have a skin which stretches around the whole world. There is never a day in which we are not stretched to a degree to which no man has ever been stretched before, no woman has ever felt before. We are evolving into a body of Christ which is not a theological concept but is an everyday experience. Never before have we had a greater capacity to stand and to experience the beatitudes. There is no description of Jesus in Scripture more lucid or clear as that found in the beatitudes. Anyone who is alive to his word today and alive to the experiences of people can describe himself in terms of those beatitudes: the beatitude of mourning, the beatitude of weeping, the beatitude of experiencing pain. The world cries out each day with a pain which we cannot ignore. Every one of us has our own pain threshhold; we can hear only so much, understand only so much, then we cut off. Humanly speaking, there is only so much pain which we can endure. Yet even after we close ourselves off, even after we hear and feel nothing further, the reality around us continues.

In reading Mark's description of Gethsemani in the fourteenth chapter, the words of Jesus, "My heart is broken" are not the words of a man in solitude; those are the words of a man who had identified himself with all mankind. And that heart of Christ is known to us in a very special way.

There is a prayer, a mysterious prayer in us. We do not know from where it comes. There is a compassion in each of us which goes beyond our own heart and our own feeling. Our technology has done something which our theology could not do. It is only in our day that we can experience an entering into the pain and anguish of all men. I was once talking with a Chinese Sister as she sat by the sea at Carmel. I saw her weeping and asked her why. She said that the ocean contained the tears of all mankind and that she could not but experience the tears of her own people. A year ago I was asked to investigate someone in one of our state hospitals who claimed to be possessed, and I spent some time with this young man. It was obvious that he was emotionally disturbed; but there was a certain clarity in what he was saying. He kept repeating, "I do not want to be responsible for Vietnam. I do not want to have the blame for the war in the Mideast." In some way, he had a deep sense of being responsible for the war all over the world; in some way, he experienced himself as a suffering servant. Later I found out that after he was released from the state hospital, he burned himself to death, one of countless victim souls who possess a transparent sensitivity to the cumulative evil which is in the world.

All of us have become aware of the new ecology, not just in terms of the physical environment but far more in terms of the spiritual environment, and we could be overwhelmed. It is readily understood why so many people are overwhelmed. No one man was ever intended to be responsible for and to absorb all of it. There is a sense of powerlessness today in terms of what is happening beyond our immediate life. We could handle private morality as it concerned the people immediately in our life. But as we become more and more aware of decisions and consequences which are far beyond anything which we can say or do, there's a feeling of helplessness, of powerlessness, of meaninglessness. Never before has man been so much in need of something beyond himself. Never before has there been such a yearning and a longing for a Redeemer, for a reconciler. Never before has there been such a hunger and a cry of the heart for someone to make sense of life. We experience readily within ourselves the need for a God of the Old Testament, a God who will vindicate himself, who will act decisively, reward and punish. Everyone is ready for a God of power, a God who can make himself felt but we are not ready, and perhaps will never be deeply ready, for the God of the New Testament, a God who embarrasses us by his helplessness, his powerlessness, by the fact that he comes as man and that he comes and continues among us hidden and silent. We are embarrassed by our God, we are embarrassed because he is a suffering God.

Among the Indians in the Altiplano of
Bolivia, there is a statue to an ancestral
god. They do not even know his name, but
one thing they do know is that it is a god
who cries. Probably one of the greatest
miracles of the New Testament is the
reality that Jesus cried. We probably have
never thought about the tears of the Father
at the death of his Son and perhaps we are
not aware of the tears that God continues
to cry because he has identified himself
with all men. "He hangs upon the cross
until the end of time in his suffering body,
mankind." Because of the evolution of
conscience and of consciousness, the corporate consciousness which we have, every
Christian is drawn into the anguish of
Christ, drawn into a Gethsemani, drawn
into a suffering. It is a suffering the origin
of which we do not know, a suffering
perhaps never before experienced, a weeping sometimes even without sign of it.
There's a word in the fifth chapter of
Hebrews which describes the Christian of
today, "during his life on earth he offered a
prayer and entreaty aloud and in silent
tears to the one who had the power to save
him out of death and he submitted so
humbly that his prayer was heard." "Aloud
and in silent tears. . . ." The Christian
becomes aware that there can no longer be
the stranger in his life, that every neighbor
is brother and sister, that every person
whom he meets is a hidden Christ. The
mystery of Eucharist, the heart of our

prayer, the heart of reconciliation means that we have heard and have listened to the words of Christ each day, not words uttered over bread and wine, but the words of the Eucharist begun over bread and wine and echoing over every person.

The Fathers of the Church describe the prayer of Jesus as the prayer which he utters to his Father from deep within our own heart. And he utters over every Christian: "This, too, is my body and this, too, is my blood." And we hear these words each day, not with our ears but in our innermost heart, making conversion an imperative. Prayer which does not lead to conversion is not yet Christian. Prayer which does not lead into deeper community has not begun to have its effect in us. There is no mid-ground between violence and reverence, between love and hate. We are each, without exception, under a command to love one another as he has loved us. The fourth gospel, written by the beloved disciple toward the end of the first century, is a depth of insight because of the lapsed experience, the cumulative experience of the Christian community. When John wrote that gospel and when he came to the Last Supper, he did not repeat the words of consecration, rather in their place he described the deepest meaning of those words. He described the mystery of Christ thus: that before he took bread and wine into his hands, he took the feet of his disciples into his hands and said, "If I your

Lord and Master wash your feet, so you too must wash each other's feet." The command of Christ to wash one another's feet; how many feet have I washed? Who is my neighbor? Who is enemy, who is stranger, who is brother? Who is friend? Who is servant? The words of relationship are a key to the Gospel. They demand an answer.

A new answer. Every word of relationship in the gospel has reference to our relationships of each day. The Christian cannot accept anonymity as final. The Christian cannot celebrate Eucharist, unless he first go to his brother and make peace. Can the Eucharist ever be celebrated? The Eucharist is a sign that we have become reconciled, that we have become one, that we have overcome the enmity within ourselves, that we have acknowledged that we are sinners, because without acknowledging that, we can never claim brotherhood. How easy to be stranger when we call ourselves disciples. How easy to say the word love when there is no love. If I do not see within myself the cause and root of all the evil of the world, then I can have no part with reconciliation. The Eucharist begins with an admission, with a confession that I am responsible for what is happening in the world, that I have come to receive power to break down the walls, the strangeness which has endured since the first Cain and Abel.

The gospel calls for unconditional love which is to say it calls for unconditional suffering. Although the gospel puts no value on suffering in itself, if one loves, then one cannot escape suffering. The very meaning of love is to render oneself present even to those who do not choose us and to continue to render ourselves present over and again. To reconcile is to heal, to forgive. We are commanded to forgive, and with a forgiveness which is far more than a matter of words. I ask myself, "Have I ever forgiven anyone? Have I ever healed anyone?" When Our Lord forgave, it was not with a word or with a gesture. When he forgave, he took whatever evil he found within a person, absorbed it into himself, and overcame it within himself. Nothing of that evil or sin remained. We have all seen fathers or mothers absorb the temper tantrums of one of their children, letting the child exhaust his anger and hostility upon them. It is far more difficult to absorb the anger and hostility of an adult because that can hurt so deeply. We are far more moved to keep peace by preventing the occasion, by separating ourselves from the very people who might touch the nerve cords within ourselves. We find it far easier to accept separation and distance, to adjust to the situation of co-existence. But that is not reconciliation, that is not where our prayer should lead us. It was Ghandi who beautifully summed up the gospel by saying, "the love of one man is sufficient to compensate for the hatred of millions."

In prayer we first become present to ourselves because it must be an "I" who stands before him. We enter into his presence and he sends us forth. All of our prayer is an effort to receive the thought and truth of our mind into our heart, and from our heart into the marrow of our bones, into our hands, into our feet. We are sent and we are to create—to create an environment, an environment of understanding, of compassion. We are to create the possibility of other people becoming present to themselves, we are to become a center of communion, of community where we cease to be anonymous, where we recognize one another as brother and sister, loving another not because we need him, but simply for himself. It is difficult to comprehend how totally we are called to create family and kinship, not just in terms of our immediate family, but in terms of every person.

Sometimes it is good to remember the old classic meditation on the four last things: death, judgment, heaven, and hell. There is nothing more real, nothing more certain. The old question: what will heaven be like? What is the kingdom to be? And we answer today, the kingdom is becoming right now. In this kingdom, we shall know each one with his own understanding, be able to love him with his own love. But this kingdom is being established right now, the kingdom to come depends upon the kingdom present. In his recent book, John Dunn describes darkness as the shadow of the earth. The darkness of this night is but the shadow of the earth. Each one of us casts a shadow. Each one of us has to become transparent in order to engender light. The paradox of our day is that never before has there been more communication, more knowledge; never before have we had more possibility of understanding, of closeness, but never before have we known more distance, more loneliness, more fear. He came into the darkness, and the darkness did not receive him. But he is the light and each one of us is light. Our most radical kind of prayer is believing, hoping, loving so deeply that almost in a boomerang effect, we become that which we believe and we experience how much we are light.

And as we read Scripture, we become more aware that it is an autobiography, that we each answer the question: "Who is Jesus?" by boldly saying, "I am." We dare to believe his promise that we can do even greater things than he had done. But there is no reconciliation without love, there is no love without suffering. That great symbol of reconciliation, the washing of the feet, is so significant for when one washes another's feet, he can not see his face. They could be anyone's feet. They could be his feet. The challenge, the confrontation of reconciliation, I think, is intended to bring us to a point of utter powerlessness, of utter helplessness, which launches us out into a new search. Our God is a God hidden and silent. He does not intrude. He does not impose; only if we ask, can we receive. Only if we seek, can we find. At times we have heard the language of spiritual theology about a dark night of the soul or of the senses. Everyone today who prays to any extent knows the experience of the dark night of ministry, of the dark night of teaching, of the dark night of reconciliation even in one's own family. What father knows his son, what daughter knows her mother, what brother can really speak to his sister, what families have ever shared their prayer together, not the prayer said in common but that deep personal prayer? Never have we talked more about freedom than we do today. But we merely talk about our pain. Freedom is a pain, a deep pain of absence. There is no freedom where there is not the spirit of Christ. Only the spirit gives freedom, the spirit of Jesus. Only suffering can lead to healing. The call to prayer leads to the sending in reconciliation, but not without tears, not without blood.

The Eucharist is the living incarnation of his prayer of reconciliation. It has all happened already. We are one. We do have freedom. Reconciliation has already taken place, but so many have not experienced it. And this is our call, this is our mission that we are to make disciples, we are to make hearers, we are to create a kinship. We are to love unconditionally whether one is worthy of that love or not. Reconciliation begins with presence. We are taught presence through the Eucharist, to render ourselves present to the people in our lives. We are not called upon to change Washington or Paris or Saigon, but each of us has a milieu, has an environment. Each one of us creates his own ecology. Each one of us has an almost unbelievable power to create one another, to call forth life. Each of us is enough energy to change a city because he is with us. A writer of children's stories, a few years ago, wrote a little book called *The Way Of The Wolf.* In one of the stories, he has this little paragraph, "Condemnation is easier than investigation. When we investigate the reasons why people act as they do, we would find that they have to act the way they do and that such action in the light of the circumstances is quite understandable and totally forgiveable and even completely reasonable and just as it should be." Everything is understandable and just as it should be! To love, to understand others as I understand myself, how long a time it will take to come to that kind of understanding. How long it will take before we can begin to be able to hear his command: "Love one another as I have loved you," before we can begin to abandon ourselves to others as he has abandoned himself to us.

Prayer of Abandonment

Father,
I abandon myself into your hands;
do with me what you will.
Whatever you may do, I thank you:
I am ready for all, I accept all.
Let only your will be done in me,
and in all your creatures—
I wish no more than this, O Lord.

Into your hands I commend my soul;
I offer it to you with all the love of my heart,
for I love you Lord,
and so need to give myself,
to surrender myself into your hands,
without reserve,
and with boundless confidence,

for you are my father.

Brother Charles of Jesus

The word abandonment has not the same meaning which we associate with Dante's "abandon all hope you who enter here," nor does it connotate the quietism or passivity of the last century. It is a word of ultimate, human freedom. There are many who are not free to pray, not free to become reconcilers because they do not own their lives, because they cannot be present to themselves. Unless I can become present to myself, I cannot become present to another. The word we speak to the Father does not become real till we can say it to those who are immediately in our lives. Christian prayer is not a relationship which says, "Lord, Lord" or "Father, Father;" it says that I become present and enter into the pain, the anxiety of the person who is with me each day. It might be good to take this prayer and in place of the word "Father" or "Lord," to see the name of the person with whom you find it most difficult to be present, see in what way you can pray this prayer to him or in what way Christ can pray this prayer in you to him. The most difficult reality we have to overcome is our own former personal judgments and prejudices. We would probably be much closer to people if we did not see them with our own eyes, if we did not listen to them with our own selective hearing, if we would believe more deeply what Christ has said to us of them. The Christian community is intended to be a model, to be a proof of this presence in us. Our greatest liability is that our communion of prayer does not become visible. It is not evident how we love one another, how we understand one another. There is no mid-ground between hatred and love, there is no mid-ground between enemy and friend. We have created a great no man's land between enemy and friend. But in the gospel, to have an enemy means that we are unconnected, that we are unrelated, that we do not acknowledge that this is my other self, that this is me. We are one body. There are no strangers, no enemies, there are no distances between us in Christ. We have to make this known and seen; it has to

become visible. And that means that we
have to take tremendous risks and that is
why intuitively we each fear prayer and
fear conversion because it is a dangerous
business. There is nothing truer in the
gospel than the words of Christ, "Unless
you die, you cannot live," not the dying of
a physical death, but the dying to the way
we see, hear, think, judge. Remember when
Pope Paul came to the United Nations and
his great cry, "No more war." Three times
he cried that, "No more war." We must
each cry out to ourselves "no more judgment" and cry out to one another, "no
more judgment." We must change but we
are unable to change by ourselves alone.

Perhaps our deepest act of faith is to
believe that we have his heart, his power to
love. The deepest act of faith is not in the
reality that God exists but in the reality
that he loves me, knows me by name, that I
have the power of his heart, his compassion
within myself. But I will never discover this
unless I exercise it. Select a person who is
in and out of your life and decide to love
him. Christian love does not consist in
finding an object who draws love from you.
Christian friendship is not an accident of
finding the right chemistry. Christian love
is deliberate, it is chosen. I love this person
not because he is worthy of my love but
because I have the capacity to love and to
call to life, to create. No one of us will ever
appreciate the power we have to give life to
one another. We are the image of God

because we have the power to believe in someone. We have the power to create life in him. There's no greater gift which we can give to another person than our time, our presence. Every person has a capacity to bring us into a new room within ourselves which has never been opened before. Every person comes to us with a key to a locked room which we will never find without them. Each one of us is capable of being actualized by every person who enters into our lives in a unique way because each one has the capacity to unfold to us that we are the image of God. Therefore I ask you to select anyone and love that person by a sure act of will and faith. Each one of us creates vibrations in one another. Each one of us creates distance or closeness, by a word, sometimes even without a word, by directing or opening up ourselves we open another person. If one sincerely admires someone, they will unmysteriously begin to open themselves. We have so much unlimited potential which we have not even begun to use. Our prayer gives us an unlimited capacity to carry his presence, to open one another to his presence. Probably the greatest anguish, suffering which people undergo is their inability to accept love. To love like this demands abandonment like Christ's.

Abandonment does not necessarily mean that you let people do evil to you. Our Lord was not taken before his hour, but when his hour came he abandoned himself completely.

No power could ever be used over Christ without his accepting it. This is the story which we find in all Russian literature. Her prophets were always martyred then they were canonized. But what price canonization! This is our very real fear, that if we open ourselves out to others, we will suffer immensely, especially from our own family. But we must take the redemptive initiative. It's not a matter for wavering. We have but to take that first step, continuing to believe in that person. Our belief, our hope, our love will then be redemptive, be healing. If however we do not believe it ourselves, then nothing will happen. Each one of us has become the person we are because of the people who believed in us, the people who loved us. We all know our own love for another because it is a total experience, but we can never know the love of another for us except in an act of faith. It is our believing and their capacity to love which enables them to grow in that love, and this is why there is no healing without suffering. It is similar to parents who have to endure and suffer through the anguish, the hostility, the unbelief within their own children. The healing takes place ultimately in their capacity to believe in, to hope in, to love their children no matter what they do. The most incredible fact is that the Lord continues to believe in us no matter where we are, no matter what we have done. No man ever weeps over his sins. He weeps because he is loved. Who of us has ever been changed or can ever be changed except by being loved. That is what redemption, that is what reconciliation is all about. But it is not dramatic, it's not accomplished in a moment or a day, it is not said with a gesture or with an embrace. The deepest kind of love cannot be felt, because it is too deep. The tactile expression of love may be merely an avoidance of a deeper kind of love. And this is where the reconciliation within ourselves is always the first step of the healing process.

Technology, like all of nature, is ambivalent in the sense that it can be used for the greatest development of man or for the devolution of man. Technology, as we so often see it, can be demonic depending upon the spirit of man. Technology in itself is a gift of the cumulative wisdom of God's providence and man's development. But its direction depends upon the human spirit. It is only in our own day that we have developed the capacity to change human nature, to change the genetic structure of man. And with atomic energy we can do such destruction. Never before have we had so much power to destroy, but it's correlative is the power to be creative.

For the first time in history man can end poverty, for the first time we can become one world. Whether this happens or not depends upon our vision, our hope, our faith. Technology had forced us to sink our roots deeper into our tradition, into our capacity to develop and to define, to find the deeper spirit within man. We did not have to develop the potential which is present within ourselves, and we would not have done so had not technology demanded that we come to handle the forces which we had released. As never before, we are compelled to use that unlimited potential which we have to create each other, to create one world. We would not do it unless we were compelled to do it. And unless we do it, the demonic will take over, darkness will envelop us. At the same time there is no cause for despair. Never before have we experienced a time of greater outpouring of his presence and of prayer. There's no question that the Holy Spirit, bent over this world and the future, depends upon our choices now. We can decide our future as never before. It is not determined, and to the degree that we discover our faith, our hope, our love, to that same degree will we determine the direction of our times. In reality it is the grace of technology which has caused us to discover our grace of presence to one another, discover our capacity to give life to one another in a way we had never dreamt possible before. One who is healthy does not choose to die or to suffer; that is never a direct choice for the Christian. Our choice is always to choose life more abundantly, to love more intensively and extensively, but in so doing, we will suffer. One cannot expose oneself to the pain and anguish in the world today without suffering from that pain and anguish. To the degree that one loves, one cannot help but suffer. The less one loves, the less one will suffer. We can insulate ourselves and separate ourselves from the pain and anguish of the world today. Never before have we been capable of isolating ourselves so totally, but in that very separation, there is a dimunition of ourselves. For a Christian, there is no option except to render ourselves present to those to whom we are sent, to the poor whether in suburbia or the inner city, to the imprisoned whether in a kitchen or in a jail, to the unfree whether it is in ignorance or in intelligentsia. But it is not a matter of choosing. No one ever chooses suffering or pain, but suffering is inevitable because of the great number of unhealed people. The closer one comes to people, the more inevitable it will be to experience their pain. We cannot do this of ourselves, but we will be compelled to follow this.

Mother Teresa has said so often that, "Christ comes to us under two forms: the form of the Eucharist, the form of the poor. Who are the poor? Only he can unfold their identity to us and unfold to ourselves how poor we are, how much is our own need." It is because of his cumulative presence and growth in us that we find ourselves with those he would be with. We are disciples because we find ourselves in the same places he found himself. We do not have to go out of our way to suffer.

That is not a Christian choice. But to the degree that one becomes present to those who are wounded, to that degree will he bleed from their wounds. This may not demand our going down into the inner city. There is no one of us who does not have within his own family someone who suffers. If families would take care of themselves, there would be no problems in the world. All of the problems of the world come out of families. It all begins there. If we could take care of our families, the world would take care of itself because the world is just a collection of broken families, of once lovers. Perhaps the most anguishing of experiences is to have a person come to us asking for help and to realize that there is nothing we can do for him, that we are not ready. In Nouwen's book, *The Wounded Healer*, there is a beautiful corollary and commentary on the suffering servant—that we are all wounded, we all need healing, and that no one can minister to another unless he is first ministered unto. Perhaps the greatest ministry we ever do to another is to allow him to minister to us, to recognize his own uniqueness. How great a ministry it is to recognize that each person has a gift to give to us, and to recognize that to the extent that we can help him to understand the reality of this gift to us, will he be free to let us be a gift to him. Therein we walk together the pilgrimage to reconciliation.

IV PRAYER IN DEPTH

When I was on my way out West, I was assigned to a seat near the front of the 747 and next to me was a little woman dressed in rather strange garb, with a small book of prayers in her hand. The little woman was Mother Teresa of Calcutta. As I looked over her shoulder, she was reading a prayer which she reads every day, as her morning prayer, the Prayer of Cardinal Newman. I had not seen it for a long time, and I think it still remains one of the classic expressions of Christian prayer. I wrote it out, and she signed it for me.

Dear Jesus, help me to spread your fragrance everywhere I go. Flood my soul with your spirit and life. Penetrate and possess my whole being so utterly, that my life may only be a radiance of you. Shine through me and be so in me that every soul I come in contact with may feel your presence in my spirit. Let them look up and see no longer me, but only Jesus! Stay with me and then I shall begin to shine as you shine, as to be a light for others; the light of Jesus will be all from you; none of it will be mine; it will be you shining on others through me. Let me thus praise you in the way that you love best by shining on others around me. Let me preach you without preaching by words, but by my example, by the catching force of the sympathetic influence of what I do, the evident fullness of the love my heart bears to you. Amen.

I cannot say much more about prayer than what is contained there so briefly and so profoundly. Prayer has wonderfully ceased to be a problem. It has become a mystery. One of our handicaps seems to be to try to turn mysteries into problems and then resolve them. I think we have come into a new wisdom and have a different kind of reverence for mysteries in which we explore further and further, know less and less, and become more and more comfortable. The mysteries have no answer; no theology will resolve them; they will never be reduced to psychology. We have become a little more ready for mystery, we have come to be comfortable with the mystery of ourselves and the strangeness of talking to God.

What an awesome thing it is to talk to God, and even more profoundly, to listen and to hear, to have suddenly experienced the finger of God. Is this madness and foolishness to those without faith? To a person of faith, there is no other way to be in faith. Each of us has come to realize that prayer is not something which is done. It is not so much in the realm of behaviour, as it is in being, being a person, being with. Prayer is not something; it is not some action of a small part of the totality which each one comprises. Jesus is prayer; and in the deepest depths of oneself, we are prayer. There is a mysterious prayer in each of us. We do not know where it comes from, but it is there. It is something like our breath. Our whole body is breathing and there is life in us which is deeper than one can sense. We are an existence of God. The prayer of adoration is becoming aware of the act of God's love creating us at this moment.

Each of us is a presence of Christ. Each of us is a gift. Our presence extends beyond ourselves. Our faith, our hope, our love connect us, put us in contact with, form a communion which we will never understand. Together we sing, "Come Lord Jesus, Come." In the last writing of the New Testament, the Book of Revelation, before those final words of that New Testament, is a promise many times unread and it is, "Yes, I am coming soon." He is already here. And it is our hope that we will begin to receive the gift, the recognition that we have already received him. Paul constantly tells us: "You have been given the Holy Spirit in order to recognize the gift that has already been given." In him we live and move and have our being. One of my experiences of prayer was along the shore of an ocean, where I experienced myself as a grain of sand wanting to possess the ocean. Someone heard my word and made it into the following poem. I think it describes each one of us very deeply:

I stand on the brink, on the edge of myself,
And wonder at all that is beyond me.
I am jealous of the ocean and the sky
    that do not seem to end
Of the universe itself that holds
    so much immensity.
I seek to comprehend all knowledge, and I
    cannot even know of all that
    has been written.
I am a finite creature.
But I ever struggle to hold within my grasp
    the mystery of being.
I want the power of knowing all, of seeing all,
    of having all,
Yet I cannot even possess myself.
I have thoughts and hopes and fears that I
    cannot often understand, nor more
    frequently admit.
I am not a comfortable creature.
Even my most cherished dreams I cannot
    make come true.
My heart cries out to me to be God, and
    my life shouts out that I am not.
And my faith is built on the hope that
    someone else is.
I am left with the experience that I exist beyond
    myself, and yet cannot contain my source.
I am a grain of sand wanting to possess the
    ocean, and the miracle of love is that I can.
He has made me so small, so he can stretch me
    to immensity.
He has made me so poor, so he can fill me,
    pressed down and overflowing with
    his richness.
He has made me so limited, so that he can
    make me boundless.
He has made me a creature, so that he can
    make me God.

He has entered my heart, and he has
    called me home.
He has called me home. "I will come to you,
    and my father will come to you,
    and we will make our home in you."

This is the mystery of Christian prayer. Prayer is something which we continually explore. We become aware that it belongs to the lost and found category. We are always losing it, but it is never suppressed; it finds us again and again. It is not that we seek and discover him, but rather that he continues to discover us. Wherever we are, he will be there. Where we are not supposed to be, he will be there also. Where can we go to escape him?

"Tell them that I go before them into Galilee, and there I will wait for them." Wherever we go, there is he waiting. We know that prayer is more than cosmic consciousness. We have been through many of the phases of the experience of prayer: the experience of nature as prayer, the deep affection of inter-personal relationships, friendship and of love as prayer. All of these are very important preambles and vestibles, entrees, hors d'oeuvres to prayer. But they are not the prayer of the Christian. Perhaps as never before we have become aware that the Christian's prayer is something new. Perhaps the most fundamental word of the Christian is newness, not just a newness for today, but an 'always' newness. There is a new creation;

there is a new man, there is new prayer. The good news will always be new; otherwise, it will not be his doing. He is absolutely inexhaustible. And this is the excitement about prayer. We have begun to discover prayer not as behavior, not as doing, not as things. We have become aware that the sounds are not prayer, the sacraments are not prayer, anymore than a menu is food or that we are nourished by looking at food. We know that prayer is a becoming and a being with. We know that prayer is much more: a mystery of him contacting us, breaking into our lives. Prayer is a revelation, a revolution, more an in-breaking of the Lord into our lives than an in-breaking of ours into his. It is a matter of being discovered much more than of discovering. We have come to know prayer as a new kind of freedom. There is much in us that is not free to pray. There is no human action which demands greater freedom than prayer. Eric Berne once said that the most basic words of any man's vocabulary are 'Yes,' 'No' and 'Wow!' No word is more difficult to say than 'Yes,' and have it a word of fidelity; to say 'No' and have it a word of fidelity; to say 'Wow' and to be lost in wonder. Because so much of ourselves is as yet unborn, so much of ourselves is yet unexpressed and underdiscovered, un-understood.

Prayer is the freedom of the sons of God, of knowing who we are. It is the freedom of knowing that there is someone who constantly reveals himself to us in the most unexpected ways. There is no experience which is closer to him than the experience of ourselves. Everything about him has to be experienced out of our own consciousness, out of our fundamental act of being which is to know and to love. It is in actualizing ourselves that we are most open to who he is; in fact it is he who must radically actualize us. Faith, hope, and love are not simply theological actions; they are anthropological actions. Faith, hope, and love in God are just the preamble to a faith, hope, and love in ourselves. He is not so much affected by our faith, hope, love, as we are. We become different persons. We enter into deeper levels of our possiblities when we believe.

Prayer is the most creative act of the human person. We have come to understand more deeply what presence is, not just all about the presence of mechanical things; the presence of light in a room, the presence of carpet or chairs; but the presence which is uniquely human. Human presence is creative and dynamic; we are like God, not simply in terms of mind and will, but in our capacity to create. Each one of us is co-creator of our lives, of ourselves, of one another. We do not simply create an environment; we create the deepest capacity in one another. Each one of us remembers words of life, words of death which have been spoken to us. No word is more life-giving than the words "I love you," and no word more devastating than the words "You are nothing." Because of our innate incapacity to believe in ourselves, we easily pick up one another's fear, one another's rejection, one another's love. Prayer is a deep act of prophecy, an extraordinary creative prophecy. In Corinthians, the fourteenth Chapter, Paul writes, "You must want love more than anything else, but still hope for the spiritual gifts as well, especially prophecy."

Self-concept is self-prophecy. We have come to understand how destructive or how enhancing our self-concept can be. We fulfill our image of ourselves. Other people will fulfill what we think of them as well. Prayer in the radical sense is believing the word of God about ourselves. All that we read in scripture is autobiographical and prophetic. His commands are prophecies. He enables us to do what would be impossible of ourselves. No one can climb the mountain when he is told to do so. One does not have the strength from a distance. It is only in the process that one discovers the capacity and develops the potential to climb the mountain.

The mountain is not outside of ourselves, it is within ourselves. We owe a great deal of gratitude to the technology of our time. We come slowly to realize that the physical, the material, the technological develops so much ahead of the deep spirit. Our technology is an expression of the spirit, but on the simple level. Never before

have we experienced a universe so far
beyond our capacity to limit. Never before
have we been so extended. Our world is far
different from the world in which Christ
lived, or in which our parents lived. The
world has indeed expanded beyond our
grasp. There is no longer one universe;
there are several universes. Research scien-
tists come to speak today of outer space
and of creation. The whole material universe has come to resemble a vast thought,
an incredible act of energy rather than
something material, something physical.
The imagery used by spiritualities of the
past are like infants' toys, cradles, distrac-
tions, compared to the imagery which is
given to us today.

We struggle with the power of evil. We
have been too familiar with phenomena
such as exorcism without realizing that
each one of us is exorcist. Each one of us
has sufficient power to overcome all the
darkness which exists. One spark of light
can overcome all darkness, but all darkness
cannot overcome the least amount of light.
It is our technology, our stretch into outer
space which has demanded of us that we
sink our roots more deeply. There is a
certain new kind of solitude perhaps never
experienced by men before. Little children
love fences. They love to climb on them,
they love to challenge them, to push them
out as far as possible, but take down the
fence and they will huddle closely to the
house. We are all afraid of the new fron-

tiers. We are all humbled in ways no man has ever been humbled before. We are overwhelmed by our power, not just over material things, but over one another. There is a contraction, but it is a contraction which happens just before the quantum leap.

Never before have we been so awed by technology, but this has contracted us into a new kind of depth within ourselves. Never before have we been so awed at the power of the spirit within ourselves, the capacity to experience the fullness of creation. There is a new experience of God which man up to this time could not experience because his God was very small. We are either enhanced by our own culture or victimized and limited by it. We have very small concepts of man, of God and of the Church; those were the things of the child. The reality is there; it is our capacity to understand and to make it our own, to grow into new capacities within ourselves. Do you know that all of outer space is but a mirror of the inner space and the inner journey to which each of us is called? Each one of us knows that our theologies have been too limited, our understanding of community too contracted. We all walk steps which have never been walked before.

We see a simplicity, a radicalism, we experience deep within ourselves the person of Jesus, the Alpha and the Omega. We possess a deeper awareness that he is the Alpha, and that whatever man may come to be, he will have already been there. We have ways of understanding Christ today which no man before us could have experienced because of the signs of our time, because of the expansion of the human mind. Just as each one knows himself differently than he did ten years ago, that he is unfinished, that he is the same, yet different, so we experience prayer differently, as freedom, as creativity, as a witness to others.

Each one of us is aware of our history of prayer. This is not so much something we do; it is not just on the psychological level. We do not have to validate our inner consciousness to anyone. No one validates that simple affirmation "I love." "I love you." "I love myself." Because no one can take that away from us. Merton said it well: Does there have to be an answer to every question? Questions are good only insofar as they are unanswerable. The things which draw men are not problems; we will take care of the problems; but it is the mysteries which are the cosmic swim of all men. The Christian knows that his prayer stretches beyond the experience of nature, the experience of the world, people.

There is a prayer in him because something has happened in his life, something due more to the fact that he is a member of the Christian community than to the fact that he was given the faith by his parents. There are many things we were told too soon, long before we were ready for them. We were given names long before experiences. Each man learns to pray in a unique way. No one has ever prayed like him before; no one will ever pray that way again. Each man speaks to God in a way in which no one has ever spoken to him before, and he renders himself present in a unique way. The Christian prays out of an experience which no one can take from him. But it is not his experience alone; it is always essentially the experience of community; an experience of otherness in his immediate life. We grow because of the people who have created us, who have been the trellis on which we have grown. We discover what is within ourselves because they have discovered it. We discover what is there; we do not create it or put it there. Ultimately we believe because we can believe, because we do believe. We do not too often bother ourselves with the question, "Am I?" "I am." There are certain axioms of life which come out of existence which are not verifiable in any other way except in the simple living of them. Each one of us affirms a tradition, but it has to become our tradition, it has to become our life. No one of us can be taught to pray, just as no one of us can be taught to be our own personality. There has never been anyone quite like us before, (many may applaud that statement) and there will never be anyone quite like us again.

There is a uniqueness to the existential theology we each possess. Our faith is incomplete, no one man has the fullness of faith, of hope, or of love. There is a mysterious kind of poverty which comes in our prayer. There is a mysterious kind of hunger which comes. There is a different kind of consciousness. We become different persons because of the prayer of consciousness which happens in our life. It is one thing to experience human love; at times this seems more than enough. Often times it appears too much. For the person without faith, human love is all there is and a great anxiety is created in our times, experienced in many popular songs, "Is This All There Is to the Circus?" Is this all there is to life? Is this all there is to love? Is there anyone else up there? There is something deep within the person which refuses to accept this as "it," as ultimate. There is a refusal to be quiet before the question, "What Is It All About?" There is a capacity within ourselves which can stretch to all the universes which will ever be discovered. In reading the stories of faith, in reading the Old Testament, the Prophets in the New Testament, something deep within ourselves is validated. We do not create it; it is the word of God discovering what is already there. There are certain intimations of immortality. There are certain intimations of something more.

What is this perverse restlessness and this search which is not satisfied? If anything, it is but a deeper longing. What is it within ourselves which is not content? What is that stretch beyond all that we can conceive? "The eye has not seen, nor ear heard, nor has it entered the heart of man." It is a startling experience to realize the capacity for God within us which nothing else can fill. When we read about the most authentic witnesses to the faith, the Saints and the mystics, those who peaked the experiences of their life within something more, they tell us of a loneliness which no literature can express. They tell us of a yearning which stretches beyond. When Paul speaks about that, he says he longs to die and to be with Christ. That is a startling statement. There is a boldness about it. For most of us, good old earth is more than we can handle. There is so much richness and diversity that I think most of us would be happy with a millenium. Just a thousand years, that would be enough. But there is a different kind of loneliness and depth. There is a new unlimitable capacity which happens when one comes to believe. There is a different kind of hunger, thirst, aloneness.

A few years ago I had a pilgrimage retreat with a small religious community from Detroit to Carmel by the Sea. We went out through Colorado. One of our first sights was the Royal Gorge on the Arkansas River. For those of you who know the Cleveland-Detroit area, there is nothing quite as exciting as the Royal

Gorge. To be able to look down a thousand feet, to walk across that bridge, the longest man-made wooden bridge over a gorge, to hear the cars tremble the bridge as we walked across, was breathtaking. To me that gorge was a symbol, something like the wound of human love. There is nothing which touches us more deeply than the wound of human love—a promise, Claudel said, which only God can keep; no human love ever fulfills itself. It only creates a greater yearning, a greater longing. From the Royal Gorge, we eventually went to Grand Canyon. It is one thing to have seen Grand Canyon in cinerama pictures; it is another to be on the edge, looking down a mile's length, realizing that it has taken hundreds of thousands of years to wear it down at the rate of a half inch every one hundred years. One could put a thousand Royal Gorges into the Grand Canyon and not begin to fill it.

To me that canyon was a symbol, something like the wound of divine love. This wound touches so deeply in man that eventually there are no words to express.

I think this is what prayer is beginning to do to many. Prayer reveals that there is the something more. Once we begin to get into prayer, we see reality in a different light, we begin to speak to those who die today, differently. Death takes on a new meaning, life takes on a new depth. Prayer is the most ultimate fact of our life because it is where we are most ultimately with ourselves. It is in our prayer that we discover truth and love. We discover something of the unlimitable mystery that exists. Prayer compels us to go out of ourselves. Christian prayer is not an enclosed relationship. There is something about Christian prayer which compels us to reach out, to realize that no one really prays alone. The prayer of the Christian becomes mysteriously intertwined with Christ. Christian prayer is not doing; it is listening. It is allowing ourselves to be created because of what we hear, because of the prophecy which is uttered over us, because every word of scripture is autobiographical, prophetic, does what it says, changes who we are. One begins to discover that God is not God in the sense in which the world religions speak about him. God is not a Christian word; he belongs to all men. There is a new word which one discovers, and the word is a reality. It is not simply a word. The word is Father—the word is Abba—because the ultimate word of prayer is discovery—who we are, which is to say who our Father is, which is to say who we are to become. Some handicaps which have existed in Christian prayer have been its metaphors; too often we have reduced father and son to psychological terms, sometimes even to the parent-child relationship.

When Jesus speaks of himself as Son, he is not speaking of himself as child, but as one who is all that the Father is. The mystery of Jesus lies in the fact that we know nothing about him because he never acted out of himself. There is no indication that he ever did his "own thing;" Christ was obedient, which means that he listened deeply, radically. The root word for "obedience" is the same as it is for the word "pray;" it means to listen. Christ prayed deeply, he listened deeply to the reality of the Father. Jesus revealed not himself, but the Father. He is all that the Father is, and what he is, he has called us to become. Jesus has radicalized our prayer because prayer is not a burden to be done, but the task of becoming not only who we are but who we are all together. The consequence of Christ's prayer was "all that I have learned from the Father, I have made known to you. Because of this, you are my friend."

The root of friendship is prayer, because the root of prayer is presence— presence to all that is. It is not easy to be present to oneself. We spend most of our time in a flight from prayer, which is a flight from ourselves. We can take only so much of ourselves; but it is only in a radical pres- ence to ourselves, in a coming to say "I am," that we can be present to him who is all that we are. Our presence to him becomes a compelling force to be present to others. We can know that we are living in him, that he is living in us because he lets us share his spirit." Open your hearts to one another as he has opened his heart to you, and God will be glorified. Each one of us has been entrusted with a gift which is intended for one another."

Whatever Christ did, he did out of the Father, so that whatever he did led him more deeply into the Father, compelled him to live more deeply what he had heard. That is the radical root of our prayer. That is the prayer of Resurrection: the Resurrection radicalized each day in the Eucharist. If he is not with us, then our faith is in vain. The Eucharist is that radical kind of presence which compels us to open to him. There is a beautiful kind of fear today, a fear about prayer. Prayer has never been taken more seriously. When anything is taken seriously, there is fear, a healthy kind of fear because this fear is the beginning of wisdom. Never before have there been more people who are afraid to pray because one never knows what will happen. Be very careful of what your prayer asks for—he may hear you. There is a fear of prayer; moreover there is a fear of the Eucharist. It is a beautiful kind of a fear because never before have so many people taken him so seriously. There is a beautiful seriousness about the Eucharist. What if it is true? Those words which he said to Martha, "Do you believe me? Do you believe my words?" What happens when we render ourselves present to his Presence? It is a good thing to tremble before the living God; I think this is where we are coming to be. It is a humbling experience. Could he who became man choose a more ordinary way to be with us?

My favorite story about prayer is one I heard this summer. One evening a priest who was visiting Ireland was walking along a country road when he came upon an elderly gentleman. As they walked along enjoying the evening together, a storm suddenly arose and they took shelter. They talked for a while, and then when the silence came upon them, the old man took out a small prayer book and began to pray. The American priest observing him was struck very deeply by a certain kind of hallowedness around him as he prayed. Unintentionally, he said aloud, "You must be very close to God." The old man paused, smiled, and said, "Yes, he is very fond of me." *Yes, he is very fond of me.* That is what prayer is all about. It is discovering. It is discovering in a very exciting and never-ending way how fond he is of us. There is that something within us which we will never quite finish exploring. Have you ever listened to the silence of another person? All the different kinds of silences we carry within ourselves! The most precious moments which people share with one another are the silences which follow deep communication in words. We have all picked up a shell and listened to the ocean. The ocean within person is far deeper, far more mysterious than the sound of the ocean itself. The poet speaks about the winds which awakened the stars now stirring within his blood. It is the ocean of silences, not the absence of noise, but the never-ending silences which we continue to discover within ourselves. It is the ocean of prayer—the prayer whose origin we do not know. How it comes; when it will come remains a mystery. It is the ocean which springs up into life everlasting, that mysterious more to us. The French poet, L'Entremont, once said, "They tell me I am born of man and woman. That astonishes me. I thought I was something more." This is not just a beautiful thought. Prayer is the discovery that I *am* something more; the other is something more.

Christian prayer is a gift. All men pray. Prayer is a biological necessity of man. Today we know that prayer is the "in" thing. We know that prayer has become ever more essential for sanity and health. There are many people who meditate an hour every morning and every night. But meditation, the esthetic experience of music, the experiences of nature: of mountain, of ocean, of desert; even the intimate experience of friendship—all of these deeply human experiences may be, and should be, open roads to prayer, but they are not necessarily prayer. We are a form of human prayer, but something totally new has happened in the Word becoming flesh, in God becoming man. In all the prayer of the world's religions, we pause before the incredible reality that God walks among man, that God is man, that God prays—

God prays! This moment we know in faith,
as Paul expressed it in Romans and as it is
mentioned in the Letter to the Hebrews.
"He continues to pray for us." He not only
died for us, he not only rose from the dead,
but he prays for us. Wonder for a moment
at this. What is it that he prays for you? He
is praying for you. The greatest consolation
we can have is that he is praying for us, he
is praying with us, he is praying in us. It is
beyond any dream we can imagine. This
mystery of prayer is very simple. Prayer is
not a thing; it is not an action. I am my
prayer. It is I at my deepest possible level
of being. It involves mind and heart, all
that I am. Prayer is the deepest act of
human freedom. It is a difficult act because
it demands presence, it demands a deep
being with myself at that place where I am
most myself. There are strong currents in
our culture against freedom. There are
many ways of escaping from ourselves, of
being lulled, there are the interferences in
our environment which prevent us from
experiencing solitude, silence, presence to
ourselves. It takes an immense amount of
energy to be with oneself, to be unafraid to
listen and to experience all that one is. In
order to pray, we must first be able to say,
"I am." "I am, and that is good." Many
people are unable to pray because they
consider themselves as nothing, as not
worth their own time, and that is very
dangerous because if one does not experience himself as worth his own time, then

whose time is he worth? The great gift of Judaism to us was a gift of the Sabbath, the gift which tells us we are worth our own time, that we are free to be, that we are to be free from all activity except that of our own freedom before him. Only in God can man be free, can he be at peace. Only God can give the gift of peace, of hope, of faith. Prayer is an exercise of faith, the faith we all know until someone asks us: "Do you believe today?"

Prayer is not words. Prayer is life always evolving, always moving. If it stops, then it is dead. Prayer is always new. It can never be repeated, just as a moment of life can never be repeated. There is nothing old in God. There is nothing past. He is always new. He is always present, and in Christ everything has become new. At every moment all of the past is recreated. Prayer is a constant experience of re-birth, of Resurrection, of new life given to us. This is the day no one has ever experienced before; no one has ever breathed this hour before now. The moment is utterly new, and in it, all of us become new. This is one of the great powers of prayer—that it is creative of ourselves. It has taken a long time to recognize that the exercise of faith, of hope, of love have a boomerang effect. They are not simply theological virtues enabling us to reach out to God with our minds. The deepest effect of faith is not in God but in ourselves. If we believe God, then it is we who change, we become the vision which he gives to us. We become the prophecy which he utters over us. We are transformed.

No one of us would ever dare to believe in ourselves as he believes in us. Our faith is more than our mind. It is creative of us. We can only become what we believe of ourselves. What he believes of us, we can only begin to dream. The boomerang effect of hope is the extraordinary, the expectation which he has for us. Did you hope today? Do you expect him? What did you expect of the day? Prayer is the deep act of hope in the reality that he keeps his promises; that he says, "I will be with you soon. I am coming." And this day he has come again, and again, and again. He is the only one who keeps his promises totally. He is the only one whom we can never exhaust. He is always present. He is always a yes, even though we are absent so much of the time, even though we are a no. He is always a presence. Yet because we have a past, he is a remembrance in us. Each one of us is a history of prayer—that mysterious presence to ourselves which enables us to come into his presence. In all of creation, we will never find anything closer to him than our own selves. There is nothing which can be experienced except in ourselves. The greatest sacrament of God and of Christ for each of us is the gift of ourselves and the mystery of his in-dwelling in us. All the different forms of prayer, of the sacraments, all of Scripture, help us to come to believe and to live that cumulative presence which he is in our lives and in one another. Intuitively we know that prayer is dangerous, as freedom is dangerous. We would all like to be innocent. It is with great reluctance that we let go of our childhood.

Prayer is not only an I-thou relationship, because the deeper we become present to him, the more he involves us with his total self, with his whole body. Prayer is dangerous because it demands change, it demands conversion, it demands presence to others. John has so clearly said over and again that we cannot love him more than we love the people in our daily life. We can never be more present to God than we are present to one another. To say that we love him while we do not see our neighbor, while we do not see the beggar at our gate, the wounds of the person next to us, is to be in a lie. It is important for us to know that prayer demands honesty, an anguishing honesty. It is good to face the untruth of our prayer, to let go the forms of prayer which are no longer adequate to where we are or appropriate to the situation of our times.

There is no area of our lives in which we lie more than in the realm of prayer, because there is no area of our lives in which we so often use words which can betray. There is a gap between what we see with our eyes and where we walk with our feet, between the head and the heart. Prayer demands great effort, struggle to take the truth of our minds, the words of our understanding into our heart, into the marrow of our bones, into our hands and feet, into body prayer. Prayer demands decision.

There are many people who are not free to pray because they do not possess their own lives. They cannot say yes or no. There will never be time to pray. To pray means that we create time, that we are able to say yes and no with fidelity, and that we live as yes and no. Each of us is a center of prayer which is ever increasing or diminishing. Because we pray, we enter into power, a power which is only equalled by his power of creation. We have the power through our presence to each other to create or to destroy, to call to life or to diminish life. The power of our faith in someone else is almost incredible. Do you remember the first time anyone spent time with you, sought you out, the first time anyone said that he liked you or that he loved you? Do you remember the time when someone said that he was unimpressed with you, that he did not think you were much of anything? The human word has created the person we are at this moment and has created the hope of who we shall become. Each one of us carries deep wounds within us because of someone else's words to us, because of someone else's faith or lack of faith in us, someone else's hope or lack of hope, love or lack of love in us. Every person in our life has in some way created us or diminished us, opened us or closed us.

Each of us has an area, has a field of energy around us. Our presence to others calls them forth or holds them at a distance. Prayer is a universal experience, but it is an experience which we never master. It is an experience which only he can teach us, one which he does teach us through one another. A great consolation of prayer is to know and experience his own words, "I am never alone."

It is hard for us to accept the mystery of Jesus. The more we become aware of him, the more of an embarrassment he becomes. The God which he reveals is a God without color, a God who is hidden, a God who is silent. We are much more comfortable with an Old Testament God who has power and vindicates himself immediately, a God who does things. There is much of us which is still pre-New Testament. We are not comfortable with a God who takes on the weakness of man, who becomes what man is in everything except sin. It is not easy for us to live the story of Job; yet Job is the prophet of our day. We can ask ourselves: "If I did not have to love him, would I; if I did not have to pray, would I?" We are not yet free; we are not yet adequately evangelized. The word of the New Testament is more the word of our mind than it is the word of our heart, of our hands, of our feet. The radical kind of prayer to which he calls us is still at a distance from us.

One of the great witnesses to faith in Germany, Dietrich Bonhoeffer, uttered it so simply, "It may cost you your life." Our prayer may cost us our lives; our presence to him demands a new kind of presence to others. Christian prayer is a deep experience of poverty, of kenosis, of being emptied out. It is a prayer with unlimited expectations, yet with no expectations. Christian prayer is a prayer of abandonment.

We cannot use the word love to translate the reality of what Christ is speaking, because the word "love" in our vocabulary has no longer the power to translate the experience of the New Testament. I think the word abandonment can best express what we are talking about. Our word love today centers on us. It is a feedback word. But the word abandonment, unlike the abandonment of Dante or the abandonment of the last century, is the word which the artist, the creative person uses to describe the complete losing of oneself and the reality that one is: the abandonment of a dancer, the abandonment of a child through its play, the abandonment of a lover to love. Christian prayer is an ordinary, simple kind of experience. It is as ordinary as bread and wine which is the body and blood of Christ.

Who dares to say the "Our Father" in the first person singular? It is easy to say "thy will be done" as long as it is in the third person impersonal. "Thy will be done" because what can we do about it anyway? "Que sera sera." Thy will be done. There is a kind of fatalism in our prayer which has nothing to do with the reality of the New Testament. To say the "Our Father" we have to translate it into our own words, into our own lives. It means simply I abandon myself into your hands. Do with me what you will. Whatever you may do, I thank you. Who dares to utter that kind of prayer? Those who attempt this prayer experience deep within themselves a terrible dread. What if he hears me?

Almost intuitively, we know the power of prayer, and we pray cautiously, very cautiously. We create an insulation. We each know how to pray. We each experience today as perhaps never before something of that warm breath of the Spirit which broods over us, nudging and pushing us. The most surprising consequence of Vatican II has been the mysterious quest for prayer. Paul VI presented Charles de Foucauld as a universal brother in that greatly ignored document on Development of Peoples, and designated him as the special patron of our time. De Foucauld, one of the great prayers, one of the most radical men of our day, described his first experience of Jesus as starvation. How many of us experience starvation for him? Yet something is whetting our appetite. There is a kind of spiritual curiosity caused by the ecological situations of our time, the awesome expansion into outer space. Never before have we had more need of the Gospel. In some ways we did not need the Gospel in centuries past because we did not have the power to so radically change man's nature and the world. But the New Testament has come of age. Unless we hear it, we are bound to lose our identity, to lose the sense of where we are called.

We are each in the midst of an immense journey. The prayers of our families, our national heritages are cumulative. We are not simply our own personal prayer, we have within us the cumulative prayer of the Church, not just of our day, but of all time. Each of us lives in a divine milieu, a field of energy, a field of power. There is in each of us a power far beyond the power of atomic energy. It has taken the whole of scientific history to unlock the energy in the smallest amount of matter. Would we dare to believe in the energy which is locked within each of us? Ten men could redeem a city in the Old Testament; ten men would have been sufficient. What if they got nine men? Would they be able to find a tenth in our midst? But in the New Testament, the Lord said the least in the kingdom of heaven is greater than the greatest man of the Old Testament, greater than John the Baptist. The love of one man, the prayer of one person, is sufficient to compensate for the hatreds of millions.

How long does prayer endure? Prayer lasts forever, no word of faith is ever lost. Our prayer continues. We are experiencing the prayer of the sixteenth century, of the twelfth century, of the first century. And we are called by our prayer. What is prayer? It is a word which makes visible the depths, the inexhaustible depths of his presence within us. In the first century, one of the Fathers of the Church said that Christian prayer is listening to the words of Jesus which he utters to his Father from deep within us. The ultimate Christian prayer is the prayer of the Eucharist, the deepest Jesus prayer, "This is my body given for you; this is my blood shed for you." There is no Christian prayer which does not begin and end in the Eucharist prayer.

The command of Christ with regard to prayer does not just say, "Do what I have done." He asks us to become his power, his presence, to become his healing word, his creative word. The litany of prayer cannot be ended because we are each a part of that litany. We each have a prayer which has never been uttered before. We each breathe as no one ever has breathed before. We each carry within us a mysterious gift of prayer.

In whom do you believe at this moment? Do you believe in his word to you, "Greater things than I have done, you shall do?" Do you believe that you are the light of the world? Do you hope? Do you expect his coming each day?—In the many different moments of each day? Did you receive the bread which was promised to you today, the daily bread for which you prayed? Did you recognize it when it came? Do you love? Are you loving at this moment? Do you love the person next to you? Are you aware of his presence next to you? Do you feel his presence in some way touching your presence? Are you aware of the mystery which is locked within him? It could be anyone. It could be Christ. It is.

It is necessary each day to spend time alone with the Lord if one desires to know him more intimately. The rhythm of our prayer is given to us by the Gospel itself. Ultimately, the reason why a Christian prays is because Christ commands it. He commands it with words, but above all, with the command of his life; and if we are Disciples of Jesus, then we must pray as he did. Luke's Gospel, the Gospel of prayer, describes over and again how our Lord went out early in the morning to pray in the desert, how he prayed the night on the hill, how he prayed alone even in the midst of his Disciples. Because we are persons, because he is a person, he deserves personal time. There is a rhythm in our lives, a rhythm which changes. There is a need to pray alone each day in order to prepare for the great Christian prayer, which is the prayer of the community, the prayer of the Eucharist.

Our celebration in community, the depth of our community prayer, depends upon our personal preparation. The community prayer, in turn, reinforces and deepens our personal prayer. There is a great need today for the day in the desert, the day alone. We have forgotten the Sabbath law and we are paying an extraordinary price. We need a day, at least once a week, if we are going to be free people. If we are going to be able to see, to respond to the Gospel today, we need time to be with the word of God. In the eighth chapter of John's Gospel, our Lord says simply, "If you make my word your home, you will indeed by my Disciples. You will learn the truth, and the truth will make you free."

When we pray, "Give us this day our daily bread," our daily wonder, he has already done that. The word of God is available to each day. The Disciple of Jesus would never go a day without hearing that word, letting it create him. The word of God is not simply a word about him. Every word of Scripture is a consecrating word; it renders him present; it renders us present to ourselves and to him. There is a deep need for the breath of God which is his word. Were he to appear in our midst visibly and tangibly, he would have no more words to say. There would be no more actions for him to do. Whatever he could have done, he has done; whatever he could have said, he has said. Christian prayer is a conversation with someone whom you know loves you. But it is never just a word in our ear; it is a conversation that comes from the word of Scripture.

Christian people feel those powerful influences when we read or pray the Scripture together—Scripture was not written to be read in isolation, but was intended to be the prayer of the group, of the family, the families of families.

It is an illusion to think that we have no time, that we are working eighty hours a week. Unless we tithe our time, tithe our presence, something happens to us; we become unfree. Prayer is not a luxury. It is the very basis of our being free to respond to the deepest parts of ourselves and to him. Perhaps as never before, in order to overcome the ecological environment of our time, the absence of silence, the inability to respond to one another, our inability to form community, our inability to be with ourselves, to be alone, we need at least one day a month, perhaps a block of time each week. We think nothing of going to a movie two or three hours, watching a football game, watching a television series, but how often do we take two or three hours to be present to him? Very often we cannot stand being with him because we cannot stand ourselves. There is a very deep need for us to do this, a psychological need as well as a spiritual need. There should be some time each day when we value ourselves enough to spend time with ourselves and when we spend time in faith's presence to ourselves, we enter into his presence. He is always there. A recent author made the simple comment that the darkness of the world is caused by the shadow of the earth. All the darkness of the night which we encounter is caused by the shadow of the earth. There is a lot of darkness which we create for ourselves because we stand in our own shadow and do not turn to the light; it is only in turning to the light that we can overcome the darkness.

If we are to increase and develop a deep prayer life, fasting is essential. Prayer, like most spiritual things, is usually in a lost and found category. Who has not lost his prayer? Who has not lost his fasting? And because these are such deep values (the deepest spiritual values are the deepest human values), we find we must now import them from the East! There is a new discovery of fasting—fasting as the prayer of the body which frees the spirit and the soul to experience itself. There is a new devotion which some of our students have begun, the forty-hour fast; there is something about the body, its very deep relationship with the deeper inner person. We sometimes have to experience that hunger of the body in order for the spirit to awaken. By fasting, some people are led into a new sense of prayer within themselves. It is a startling moment to reach the point when you know that if you do not eat, you are going to die. It is a startling moment to realize that you could die from not eating. It is a rare experience for most Americans, but I think it is an important one because we begin to realize how much everything is gift.

The Christian prayer is essentially Eucharistic. It is essentially an experience of joy; it is the discovery of the gifts of the Holy Spirit and the fruition of that spirit in us which compels us to live with these attitudes. The spiritual life is simply discovering that we do have a Holy Spirit who works within us. It is striking to meditate the Eucharistic prayer, where over and again the expression "by the working of the Holy Spirit," is repeated. He has given the Holy Spirit as his first gift to those who believe. Did you ever wonder about his second gift? Or his tenth gift? It is the person next to you. The greatest gift next to the Holy Spirit is that person next to you—the people in your everyday lives. All of the sacraments are intended to educate us to the tremendous truth that the ultimate sacrament, the ultimate effect of the sacrament of Jesus is that we become sacrament, to ourselves, first of all, and then to one another. Those who pray deeply will ultimately find themselves fasting. When one prays, when one begins to discover one's unique grace of prayer, one's taste changes; one's sense of time is changed. Prayer radicalizes; prayer frees. Most of us are terribly unfree. When one prays faithfully, things which were formerly important to us lose their importance—people change, because something happens when we allow ourselves to live in his presence—we become more conscious that his presence is in others.

Prayer is a way of rendering ourselves present to ourselves, and out of that presence, to enter into his presence, and in his presence to be taken into the presence of the whole Christ. When we say "Jesus prayed," we mean that he rendered himself present to us and continues to do so. What happened at that Last Supper, when Christ said, in the presence of his Disciples, who recognized his presence, he said, "This is my body given for you." How do you do the Eucharist? How do you pray the Mass? There are no spectators. No Christian can be a spectator. It is not something to view or to see. The only way a Christian can celebrate Eucharist is by doing it. The Christian experiences deeply his poverty in prayer. There is no one who experiences his own prayer poverty more deeply than the priest, the leader of prayer for the Christian community. Day after day he must say, "This is my body given for you. This is my blood to be shed for you." So many of those words are double-edged. They are the word of Christ; they are also the command that we become that word. Jesus himself could not utter these words over his Disciples. He could not say these words over us; no priest can say these words over another human person.

Regardless of how much he longs to give his life to be able to change one man's mind, one man's heart, he cannot do so.

The ultimate call of Christian prayer is the use of our freedom, is to be able to utter the words of consecration over ourselves. No one, not even Christ himself, can say that prayer. Each one of us, each day, begins again to do that consecration of ourselves of our lives—this is my day, my life, my work given for you. We cannot do that of ourselves. Only Christ can pray that prayer. But each day, every time we pray, we draw into ourselves ever more radically his presence, his power. Prayer is a power.

In comparison to that power, atomic energy is but a penny candle. We will never adequately understand the power, the creative power of God himself which is given to each of us, the power of love, the power of hope, the power of faith, the power of healing, the power of changing. May the first miracle to be myself. Jesus' prayer, Jesus' promise, "I am with you always," is kept. We can only express our open desire to be present as he is present.

"If you but knew the gift of God and who it is that speaks in you." Listen for a moment to the sound of your own name. Every time that we hear that word, the word we use least frequently of all, we are not free, we are compelled to respond. Everyone calls our name differently. One man says our name, and immediately we break into joy. Others may say our name, and we respond, "Oh, no." Who is the one, who says our name most deeply? Who calls us most deeply to life? How does he call us by name? Remember the words of Isaiah, "I have called you by name. You are mine. I forbid you to be afraid. Be at peace. I am with you." Be aware of how he is called, how Abraham, David, Isaiah, the patriarchs, the prophets, how Mary was called at Nazareth, John from the desert, each of the Disciples and the Apostles, how he has called our name from all eternity. Our parents did not know what we would be. They had an alternate name just in case. But he knew us before even our parents, he had called us and has never ceased saying our name because we are a word which he has not finished uttering. There is much unknown, uncreated in each of us; and each day he calls us to new life, to new possibilities. Try to hear how he says our name. Listen to his word. The word of the Eucharist each day: "I abandon myself into your hands. Do with me what you will. Whatever you may do, I thank you. I am ready for all. I accept all. Let only your will be done in me and in all your creatures. I wish no more than this. Into your hands I commend my body and my blood. I offer all and each, for I love you, and so need to give myself, to surrender myself into your hands without reserve, and with boundless confidence, for you are mine."

No one has ever believed in us so totally, so completely. No one can ever express a deeper hope. We are being loved now as totally as we can ever be loved in eternity;

it is our human overcast which prevents us from experiencing this kind of love. He comes hidden, silent. He comes humbly because he will not overwhelm us. He speaks each day, but we cannot listen, we will not hear unless we desire, unless we long, unless we hunger and thirst. We must become aware of how our presence extends beyond ourselves to all other persons in our lives.

Whenever I see the Tomb of the Unknown Soldier, I think of the unknown saint, the unknown saints in each city. I think today of the unknown Theresas and others like Francis, of the unknown holy people who brush against us each day, the communion of prayer, the communion of saints. Would it not be sad to have been with them for an hour of prayer, never to have shared a word with them? At the Last Supper, our Lord said, "All that I have learned from the Father, I have made known to you. Because of this, you are my friends." You are my friends. How unique is Christian friendship because we have shared what we have heard and learned from the Father. We can know that he is living in us and we are living in him because he lets us share his Spirit. Open your hearts to one another as he has opened his heart to you, and God will be glorified. Paul says for all of us, "I have been entrusted with a grace that is intended for you."

Listen to the words of Colossians, that marvelous letter of prayer, that testimony of faith of Paul (Colossians *1*,27): "The mystery is Christ among you, your hope in glory. This is the Christ we proclaim. The wisdom we thoroughly train everyone and instruct everyone to make of all full grown in Christ. For this I struggle wearily on, helped only by his power, driving me irresistibility." Paul says all those other things and yet they were only pale reflections of what was coming. The reality is Christ. And then he says: "There is only Christ, he is everything and he is in everything." We must become aware of our capacity to believe, our ability to hope because we have already received something of the promise, our capacity to be loved and to love. It is not that we go to him, but rather that he comes to us each day. "The Lord Yahweh has given me a disciple's tongue. So that I may know how to reply to the wearied, he provides me with speech. Each morning he wakes me to hear, to listen like a disciple. The Lord Yahweh has opened my ear" (Isaiah *50*,4). He awakens us. He hatches us into a deeper consciousness of who he is, of who we are. To listen to him is to be stretched to his dimensions, to enter into the fullness of his body, to enter into the fullness of our own center.

The writer of the Book of Revelation, the Apocalypse, puts it so clearly and so succinctly. "Here is the message of the Holy and faithful one who has the key of David, so that when he opens, no one can close, and when he closes, no one can open.

I .know all about you. And now I have
opened in front of you a door that no one
will be able to close, and I know that
though you are not very strong, you have
kept my Commandments and not disowned
my name. I have opened in front of you a
door which no one will be able to close."
Thanks be to God (Revelations *3*.8).

V APOSTOLIC PRAYER: PRAYING IN THE MIDST OF WORK

My understanding of apostolic prayer is rooted in the words of Our Lord that we are to pray always. In the past there has been a tendency to compartmentalize prayer and apostolic life. We tended to think of prayer apart from our work. Then we came to discover work as parallel to prayer. And now perhaps the most significant revolution is happening in our own day. We have come to discover that we cannot simply pray one hour a day or four hours a day; that would not be adequate. As Mother Teresa says: We must pray twenty-four hours a day; our whole life must be a prayer. In the past, there has been a tendency to think of prayer as a mental process or a process of moving the lips. We are familiar with the "Jesus Prayer," "Lord Jesus Christ, Son of God, be merciful to me a sinner," but it is impossible to say this all day long. We are aware that we cannot pray in the traditional way all day long nor can we substitute our work for our prayer. We have been caught in a dilemma for a long time: How does our work become our prayer? And how does prayer penetrate our whole day. I do not pretend to have the answers but I think there are certain ways we can explore together. One way is through the prayer of listening. We cannot always do this consciously but there can be something of an expectancy that he will be with us and a gradual unfolding of faith, hope and love during the day. One method of consciousness examen at the end of the day is to reflect on how did I believe today, hope, love? What were those moments during the day when I was conscious of being in faith, in hope, in love.

In the past there has been a tendency to identify prayer with verbal forms. We made an act of faith because we said the words. We can no longer limit prayer to words, place or time. Prayer is the hope, the expectancy that he will be with us today, a kind of Zaccheus experience. Zaccheus was anxious to catch a glimpse of Jesus that day. And the most important part of that story is the last line when Our Lord said that he was sent to the lost tribe of Israel. Zaccheus had never seen Our Lord; Our Lord had never seen Zaccheus, but he knew his name, he called him by name. Zaccheus was in the tree for one reason. The Lord had been calling him, had been drawing him there all the time. It is important to realize that there is something within us which goes beyond ourselves, an interior experience of him who is drawing us before him. Our Lord at the time of his resurrection said to Mary Magdalene and the women: "Tell my disciples that I am going before them into Galilee and there I will await them." Wherever we go, he will have already been there. He is continually drawing us. No one can go to the Father unless Jesus enables him to do so. No one can go to Jesus unless the Father draws him. We have to let ourselves activate what I call a prayer field. In physics there are certain fields of energy, certain polarizations. In a similar way, we have to be more aware that we are in God's field of prayer, God's field of providence and that there is never a moment when he is not present to us even though we are but rarely present to him. Chardin made famous that expression, "The Divine Milieu." I think we have to be much more conscious of what we can call the "Eucharistic Milieu." He is always present in our lives, always calling us to a more explicit, conscious awareness of his presence. We have all had certain moments of this sixth sense, or what some call a second consciousness. This is an operation of the Holy Spirit, an activation of his gifts. It is something like mystical prayer not in the same degree as John of the Cross or Teresa of Avila but there is what we can call, for want of a better word, a mystical consciousness, mystical: meaning something that he does which is beyond our own activity.

To those who are honestly seeking him, this is not extraordinary at all. In grade school we learned about actual grace, moments of remembering God. The Jesuits have helped us greatly in the rediscovery of the discernment of spirit. There is never a moment of the day when we are not being acted upon. At this moment there are literally hundreds of things going through our minds, pulling on us. If we were able to read a stream of consciousness it would be something like one of the Italian streets; our minds are like the Via Appia. There are hundreds of thoughts going on inside of us at any given moment. We select but one or two. We are living in a very crowded consciousness. Some thoughts are totally neutral; others are grace-filled; still others are of the ungraced spirit. We are continually bombarded by the whole ecology of environment, by the effects of all of our previous history—all the things going on in our minds and hearts, all the pressures which build. But there is also the activity of the Holy Spirit, Father and Son going on in us at every moment. He is always with us; there is never a moment when he is not with us. The sun is always shining even though the earth at times moves away from the sun. It is our human overcast which prevents us from seeing him. On a clear day we can see forever. Some days we cannot see beyond our nose. Some days we are totally locked in ourselves. Some days we want to smile but we cannot smile; we are frozen within. But there is a continual movement in us toward a deeper consciousness.

Never before in the evolution of human consciousness has there been as much overexposure, overexperience as we have today. We find ourselves growing with a new capacity, a new unity of vision which no one has had before. We have a consciousness of God today not through mind-blowing efforts but through a gracious remembrance of him. We find this in the documents of Vatican II—our various ministries are sources of our spirituality. In our ministry, we are doing the work of Christ, in some way we are rendering Christ present and this should be sanctifying. It is not only when we pray in isolation that we are sanctified, our work during the day is sanctifying. My prayer might make up but one hour during the day. What of the other twenty-three hours? How much time do we spend at Mass, at prayer? When we reflect upon it, it is but a small fraction of the day. Is Christ just as present during the remainder of the day? It is good to remember that the Mass may not necessarily be our most conscious experience of Christ during the day, nor our highest activity of prayer. Sometimes the greatest experience of poverty for a priest is the Mass. Prayer is not simply doing holy things, holy actions; we can do all things in the spirit. And we grow into the gradual awareness that whatever we do can be done in him. In our listening, our discerning, he is always present to us. So much depends upon our looking for him, our expecting him with the assurance that today he will be with me. He promises to be our daily bread. How good at the end of the day to ask ourselves: "What bread did he give me today?" We have to collaborate with this transparency. It is something like those puzzles we used to see in the Sunday papers—figures in the maze. He is always there. Perhaps we would recognize him if we could develop a certain kind of ear, a certain kind of eye—the inner eye, the inner ear attuned to that presence which is always there. It is a matter of training, developing, cooperating with the graces which are always there just as one develops a certain appreciation for music through instruction and training. How much do we really desire to catch a glimpse of him? How deep is our desire for conscious communion with him. It is unreal to expect this twenty-four hours of the day but perhaps a being conscious with him three or four times a day. It might simply be the traditional prayer of aspiration "God is good," "Thank you."

The Japanese have a beautiful custom of making a profound bow with a certain delicacy of movement. They bow before a flower, even a grasshopper. For them, it is a profound act of gratitude. This is the second stage of conscious communion, that we develop a gratitude for life itself, graciousness toward everything that is. Like the nine lepers, we forget to be grateful to the one who cured us. Nine-tenths of the time we forget; our greatest enemy is amnesia. We need to develop a Eucharistic spirit. We say grace before meals. Why not before we take a shower, or hear someone sing, or when we receive a letter? Chesterton was known to say grace when he took a walk, took a shower, or ate an apple. Everything is grace. Everything is worth our gratitude; everything is gift: health, talents, friends. We take so much for granted. Our spare moments should be a turning inward in gratitude; "Sursum Corda," lift up your heart in thanksgiving.

How do we stay in thanksgiving? Grow in love? What do we do when we find someone who is not lovable? How much power we have to choose, to select even those who are not impressed with us. Unfortunately in America we are caught in the consumer culture: we want something only if it can do something for *us*. This is contrary to the spirit of the gospel. What can I get out of it? Apostolic prayer is based on a deep theological truth: He is in our life. Where we are he wants to be. We can grow and develop an even greater explicit consciousness, not of the mind but of expectation, an exercise of faith, of hope, of love, knowing, hoping, in a spirit of adoration, in a spirit of surprise.

Another stage of consciousness development is the exercise of remembering. Our Lord wants us to remember the good things he has given to us. Our problem today is that we have no time to remember. To grow in this consciousness demands that we make decisions and be faithful to them. It means saying "No," and admitting that we cannot do everything. There is a tendency in us to want to do everything, if not all at once, then at least soon afterwards. How frustrating this overchoice, overexperience! We need to create time in our lives to lift us into his presence. Our apostolic effectiveness depends on our experience of God, our experience of Jesus, not just theologically or rationally, but our coming to know him experientially. And this takes time. Sometimes it takes a longer time, sometimes a shorter time, but our experience of ministry has to be an experience of him. Our ministry does not consist in what we leave of ourselves with others but in what we leave of him. What do we receive: the knowledge that our very ministry to people is an unknown presence of Christ. Every person is an existence of God; every person brings a gift. In some way this draws us to give something of ourselves. Every time we are with another person we are depositing our presence in him. We imprint something of ourselves in each other radioactively—word-prints, hand-prints, love-prints, forever. Why do we remember each other? What is there about another that I remember? Every time two people meet there is an imprinting of one in the other. The me in you remembers the you in me. I remember me in you. Much like a movie projector, we touch one another with our eyes, with light waves. We imprint ourselves on another just with our eyes. We imprint ourselves upon each other just by what we think of others. We each have vibrations about the other; we develop a sixth sense, a radioactive field for people, a real "feel" for others.

There is a certain cumulative experience which happens because of the Eucharist. Day after day anyone who is deeply in Eucharist has a new capacity for experiencing his own and another's presence. In the measure that Christ imprints himself upon us each day, so there comes to be a certain at-ease-ness with others; we have a certain comfortableness, an at-home-ness with each other because of the Eucharist. And we can actually work on this, desire this, build upon this. That is why it is important to write. Writing creates time for us to discern, to listen, to remember, to be aware of those moments when he has been with us during the day. In front of our seminary in Detroit there is a boulevard. The street is shaded and it is only at the corner, at the intersection that one gets the full light of the sun. I have often compared this to the way a day goes. It is only indirectly that we catch a glimpse of him during the day. It is only at special moments that we have a full view of the sun. There are times during the day when we try to be conscious of him but there are also those times, unchosen by us, when he is present to us. He chooses to be with us and sometimes he is with us unexpectedly. He is always where we should be. He is always where we should not be as well. When we least expect, he is there giving himself to us. There is a certain kind of third presence, an interaction going on which creates something beyond us. How are we at prayer right now? Are we aware of a presence which is more than a cumulative presence of ourselves. We need to listen to our own words. We never know what our next word will be. My twin is ever with me, my other self. And this awareness can become ever more conscious. It will call for a more intense prayer, for more prayer. A priest friend of mine once remarked that he had never given the sermon he had prepared. But he said that had he not prepared, he would not have been ready to listen at the time that he spoke. We have a tendency to reduce prayer to one key on the keyboard. Anytime is the time for prayer. We are in union with him all day long. We had better be for if we are not in union with him, then with whom are we in union?

The psalms rose out of the daily life of the Hebrew people. They were an expression of the flow of the day, of the experiences which made up each day. We should each be working on our own psalm book, reflecting back upon our day in psalm fashion, recalling, replaying, re-celebrating the daily bread which he has promised to give to us each day. In the actual moment, we do not remember, but when we look back, we say: "If I had only responded this way." We must remember our day. There is a cumulative experience in writing our psalm. The next time we have that experience it will be that much richer; we will have learned something because we will have made it a part of ourselves. If we were to write one psalm a year, we would have a good psalter on its way.

There is yet another way to pray our work and this is to pray in terms of one another. A few years ago I was suggesting small fraternal groups of five or six people but they were not that easy to gather. Today I would speak in terms of two or three, even one other person, a pusher, one to whom I am accountable. Our Lord never sent anyone out alone. He always sent them in two's, two by two. We need to rediscover the law of the gospel and share our prayer with someone. In order to grow in prayer, one needs another person, someone to be brother or sister, something like a center for discernment, decision, fidelity. We have no lack of good will. Our greatest weakness is forgetfulness. We have to make our prayer more visible, our life more transparent. We need someone to help us to be faithful, to be obedient to our own inner grace. We are continually receiving a deep inner grace far beyond what a community can give to us and we must be faithful to this grace. We so easily forget; it is so easily lost in the shuffle. We need someone to bring us to this.

We have to keep the law of the Sabbath. He asks of us the tithing of our time. He does not need our time; we do; otherwise, we will not be free. To ignore the Sabbath is to render ourselves enslaved. "He who works without prayer is a slave." (Mother Teresa). We need to review and to anticipate our lives, what has been and what is to be. We need someone with whom we can celebrate our inner lives. Where two or three are gathered together in his name, something special takes place.

Father William Johnston has used the term "vertical prayer," and he means not the prayer of words, or even of thoughts, but the prayer of presence, a qualitative presence. This kind of presence is an openness something like the photographer who is always at work in terms of what he will see; the poet who is always at work in terms of waiting for the moment of inspiration; the lover who is always ready in terms of the moment of thinking about his beloved or the moment of meeting. This is a quality of life, an attentiveness to the one love, the consciousness of the loved one which comes back again and again like a melody, a piece of music which echoes, lingers in our memory.

To say the "Jesus Prayer," "Lord Jesus Christ, Son of God, have mercy on me a sinner," is not so much a matter of saying words as it is a task of allowing each word to become so significant that it becomes a part of our very breathing, embedded in our very heart. The task of prayer is to lead us into presence, a presence to and a presence for, a readiness, an availability so that no matter what we are doing, no matter where we are, there is an ongoing consciousness, an ongoing awareness of him who has made his home in us.

VI CONTEMPLATION: HUMAN EXPERIENCE OF THE LOVE OF GOD

Love is the power to see and the willingness to fulfill the true needs of another. I prefer to call the word "abandonment" rather than "love" because love has come to mean I am the center, whereas agape puts the other person in the center. Love is the gift of oneself. Abandonment is the power to give ourselves to another. Our love is a gift of oneself. This is the glory of the human heart—that it is capable of giving itself to others. This is the moment when we are most like God because God is diffusive of himself. He has the capacity to empty himself out. In a mysterious movement we are able to empty ourselves for others. There is a rhythm in our giving. There is a vast capacity to fill. We have to love. We have to experience love. We love little children. They draw out of us the best that is within us. This is parallel to the mystery of God coming to us as a child. We are so defenseless before him in terms of the aspirations of the human heart.

In loving the Son, the Father at the same time loves the men whom his Son united to himself in his death and resurrection. *Love* becomes *eternal life*. When we speak about life, the life to come, we are simply speaking about the love which God has for us and our love for him. John has some rather puzzling statements in Chapter 17—". . .those whom the Father has given to him." Mysteriously we are a gift which the Father gives to the Son and then in turn we become the gift which Jesus gives to his Father. In the III Eucharistic prayer we pray: may we be an everlasting gift. . . that we actually become a gift to the Father, that we are the fruit of Jesus' love as Jesus is the fruit of the Father's love. It is the sign of the active love of God in our souls if we love others. The way that we know he is living in us and we are living in him is that we share his spirit. . .that we share his word, that we share that love. This is why community is so significant and why community will always be the hall-mark of the gospel. Where people come to live together, there is no reason for them to live together except that there exist a Spirit greater than the sum of the individuals.

This is why community will always be the special sacrament of God's presence, an even greater sign than the Eucharist. The Eucharist, in itself, cannot speak. The Eucharist is a sacrament of faith, whereas the community is a sacrament of the world. Community speaks to all people, whereas the Eucharist cannot speak, just as the word of God cannot speak unless one has faith. There are sacraments which are only manifest within the faith; there are other sacraments which are visible to all the world. They are moral miracles. That the church survives is a moral miracle. There is no reason to account for the church surviving so long other than the reality that the Holy Spirit sustains her. We would long ago have perished as does every other human institution. A loving community, not just a community, but a loving community in which you can find love, peace and joy is the sacrament of God's presence. A Rabbi once spoke of visiting a convent as one of the greatest experiences of his life. There he found total love, the total joy and peace of a loving community. It is a sign that Christianity has something to say. To experience what touches most deeply in a convent, in a loving community of sisters is a greater preaching to the people than the preaching of many words.

If we are careful to put this love of the Father into all that we do, it is a sign that the Spirit of Love which unites the Father to the Son is in us also and is shared by us. What unites the Father to the Son is his love, a love so intense, so deep that it becomes a person. When there is a community of people who love very deeply with great intensity, there is a 4th dimension, almost visible; one can almost taste something of his presence there.

We can speak of the spirit of a family. Every family has its own unique spirit and it is something which one can almost taste, can almost touch. We do not want anything more; we are filled. He is that real. We can never have enough of this Spirit—the *toda nada* of St. Theresa. His mercy, his love endures forever. Nothing can diminish his love, he has enough love for each of us until the end of time. This year the world population will touch 4 billion. That is a staggering thing when you realize you are one four billionth of human kind. That is not much consciousness, one four billionth! One thinks of his own consciousness and how far it reaches into the world! Yet his love is sufficient to reach out and to embrace each one of us—for us—for all time. The ministry of the love of God, then, can embrace four billion. The love of each person for us has its origin in his love, that concentration of God's love, his presence *in* everything. There is only Christ and in every person who touches us most deeply there is his Presence. Wherever we are, whatever we are doing, we are the presence of Christ. Where can we go to escape from him?—the beautiful Psalm 138 which Francis Thompson incorporated into the "Hound of Heaven." He loved us first; there would be no love at all if he had not initiated it. If there is only love in us, then we know that there is something of God in us. Even in the most hardened of sinners there is some love otherwise there would be death.

Even life itself, the breath of life, is something of his presence. Deuteronomy discovered that the love of God is obedience to the law—in response to the Old

Testament sense of Law as light and truth. Christ came not to do his own will—this mysterious surrender of our own will. It is in keeping the commandments that love is verified which is to say that there is a deeper love than my own love, there is a deeper desire than my own desire, that in responding to him I yield to a greater love. This is the essential problem: if we do not have a sense of his love then we must hang onto our own love no matter how small it is, we must. It is like the old Aesop Fable of the sun and the wind trying to take off a man's coat. The wind blew and blew and the more it blew the more the man held the coat to himself, hanging on to the little piece within himself. Then when the sun came out, shone warmly upon the man, his coat fell off automatically because he felt a greater warmth in the sun than he did within himself. So it is with ourselves, we hold onto people like the little warmth within ourselves as long as we do not have the faith for that which is beyond. It's something like the dawn—the gentleness of the dawn which breaks upon us drawing us out of the darkness. We automatically turn to light as do flowers in the window.

It is in keeping the commandment that love is verified. To love God as Father with trust and confidence; to love all men as our brothers is the sole sign of the true love of God. To love God and our brother is more than a response to an imperative; it is to be drawn to this spontaneously as a plant is drawn to the sun. It is to be drawn to be faithful, to be the constant heart—the image of the bridegroom—the wedding banquet—that kind of love, spontaneity, that kind of depth, that kind of unlimitedness. Love is not looking for the return gift. Love is the giving. And so it is a good thing to ask ourselves: how do I love? Whom do I love? How do I want to be loved?—To let our wildest imagination free. How do I really want to be loved in my heart of hearts—it is only when we know to some degree how we want to be loved that we come to know how we should love. No imagination can begin to touch the kind of love which is given to us—the kind of love he wants us to experience. Our hearts have an intuition of this kind of love and they are restless till they rest in him.

We are called to love everyone beyond distinction, beyond our spontaneous prejudice whether they be liberal or conservative, fundamentalist or rationalist, Marxist or capitalist, to love all with his love—the 26 year old and the 76 year old, the most attractive and the least attractive. Love is not situated in the outer perimeters of the human person but at the inner depth. There's a limitation to friendship. Friendship most often falls short of his love, that love which calls us to let go of the selfish self, which tends to hold on to others, which tends to cultivate some and be non-responsive to others. Love is the free exchange of gifts, the personal gift of each.

True love celebrates as no other can, the difference between love and sex, the difference between the physical and the spiritual,—something like the wound of human love, the wound of divine love,—the difference between the Royal Gorge and the Grand Canyon. Divine love is inexhaustible; we cannot even begin to understand the love with which he loves us now. It is difficult for us to believe that we exist solely out of his love, that our total existence is rooted in his love for us. It is love which keeps the world alive. All the popular songs express this truth but they do not go deep enough: "Ah sweet mystery of life at last I've found you," "What makes the world go round is love sweet love"—The phrases may be simple but they are on target. We are more than an act of nature or an accident. We are not just a statistical probability; we have each been chosen to be in existence. Within each of us exists an act of love. We are each an existence of God. We are each a visibility, a manifestation of love.

How does God love? We have just to look around. This is the love of God. We are each the love of God. We could each write our own history of love—What do we know about love? If anyone should be writing True Confessions it should be us, what we have come to know about love. We each have a secret—a secret which no one else knows because he loves us in a unique way. He has a different word to say to each of us. Sometimes we experience embarrassment because we say the same words to each other. We wish there were other words. We are so often limited in what we have to say. But what do you say when there are no more words. The secret word which we each carry within ourselves is that we are loved uniquely. We are each a whole new species, we are not just one among a thousand other roses. We differ as star does from star, as planet differs from planet. Can we even begin to imagine what God has done for us? Each one of us has a unique story. One is a Beethoven's 5th Symphony. Another. . .if we were put to music how would we sound? How much poetry there is in each of us, inexhaustibility, creativity. I remember visiting the studio of Sr. Helene, a Franciscan Sister in Milwaukee, and being impressed with so much creativity in one little sister. Imagine if we had the time, the number of symphonies we could write, the volumes of poetry—limitless. We could fill the Colosseum if we had enough time. Amazing grace: when we have been here 10,000 years, what we could do! What have we learned about love? About service? How often do we remember only ourselves, our own convenience. How often do we think about humility? About the last place? There is a lot of room at the bottom—Up the down staircase or down the up staircase. Do you ever try to go down an up escalator? How are we going to wash feet?

What kind of a foot washer are we? What kind of a waiter are we? Who are the people who have loved us the most? On our list of lovers, who has loved us the most? On how many lists do we find ourselves? If the Lord would let us pick our jury on the last day, if we could pick our twelve?—and how many would choose us to be on their list? Who have loved you the most and who are the most loving people you have met in your life? Who are the great lovers? I often imagined Adam looking at Eve and saying: "only one?" Perhaps Eve had the same thought about Adam.

Who are the most generous, who are the most thoughtful people who have graced your life? And the hidden love. . .how many Cyranos have you had in your life? Remember Cyrano—he withheld his word of love. How many have looked upon you in a distance, loved you—and withheld their word? How many have you looked upon in love without expressing that love? There is a certain perversity in our human love. Many times those we love most dearly see us the most infrequently, and those we do not particularly care for are continually with us.

I have been impressed many times by the retired Sisters in a community. They seem to have a secret service, a special grace for doing things which are scarcely noticed by anyone. And their delight seems to be in direct proportion to the hiddenness with which they do it. What is our secret service for the community? What is the unknown service, the unknown kind of love, the hidden love which is so much more beautiful than the love which attracts attention, the love of firecrackers and shooting stars. It is just the simple kind of quiet enjoyment. We never really realize how much we have been loved until we begin to love. One of my friends has a beautiful story about a three year old who came to her mother and asked, "What is love?" and the mother, who was a very wise woman, replied, "That is the way I feel about you," and so the little girl was very happy because now she knew what love was. When she entered the first grade there was a curly haired boy who sat next to her and smiled at her, and she would smile back at him; then she knew what love was. The story goes on. Her first date—"now I know what love is"—and when the day came when the boy proposed to her: "now I know what love is." And then when she had her first child, she said, "now I know what love is." And then when she saw her family gathered around her as she lay dying she said, "now I know what love is." And finally when she went before her Heavenly Father she heard: "Now you know what love is."

So often we wonder, "do we know what love is?" No, we do not know what love is. We will not know how much we have been loved until we see him—him in whose image we have been made. Have you ever wondered what he will look like? Do you have some image? Someday we will see him face to face. Will we recognize him. Will he recognize us? Will we be disappointed, or will he be disappointed? I once experienced a simple intuition of what that might be. One day I was laid up with a leg injury from a football accident. My mother came to visit me and the light coming over my shoulder shone directly on her face. I never had looked so long into her eyes. They reminded me of someone but I could not remember who it was. It was only after she had gone home that I realized that her eyes had reminded me of my own eyes. I had never realized that I had her eyes. When we meet him,—will there be something terribly familiar about him? Will we have his eyes? Will there be something? Someday we will see ourselves for the first time. When we look into a mirror, we cannot really see ourselves, and no photograph can do us justice. We will see ourselves for the first time because we will see ourselves as he has called us to be and it is good to look on this possibility. How much he waits for us. We tend to think that we wait for him. How infinitely patient he is year after year. How long will it take us to realize the reality of who he is. What must be his joy all along the way. To make a conversion, to make a disciple is an extraordinary experience—to have someone come to you, desire to know your secret is a healing experience which takes place because someone has loved us. Each person has a different capacity for community; each person has a different capacity for love. The exceptional child in a family can bring forth the greatest in love, or the greatest divisiveness.

God's love for us is like the love of a parent. He loves because there is no one else to love us. His special presence is love for the poor—those who cannot invite us to their table in return, the blind, the deaf, the dumb, the crippled. What kind of response do we have for the least attractive?, for the person least impressed with us? Everyone wants to be special some-time,—every child wants to be the only child sometime during the day. Our believing, our hoping, our loving is a creative act. There's a prophecy we utter over every person. If a look can kill, a look can create. By our love we can do something for a person. By our response, we can do some-thing. There is the prophetic expectation—to choose someone, to pray for someone. How we create! There is the need to play with people. It is one thing to pray with them, another to play with them, to bring out the little child, to be all our years, to be able to live all the years we have already lived. How do we initiate friendship? How do we convert? The little Prince style: "you are so valuable because of the time we have wasted together." Think of all the time we have wasted together. We become responsible forever for the rose which we love. This is such a beautiful Christian intuition, the cumulative presence which we are. Be very careful of the friends you select because you may begin to look like them. Our presence is very creative of each other—and we come to look like each other. We have to be very careful. In the book *Gift From the Sea* the author refers to the people who wash up upon our shore. Love knows of no greater devotion than of the shore to the ocean. We are all like beachcombers waiting for the gift which he washes up upon our shores each day. The dynamic of love: why do we love another? And why does he love us?—being drawn, attracted to beauty, goodness, spirit— drawn to a person's need and service—for joy, fulfillment, exhilaration. All of this leads into worship; ultimately love becomes worship; worship becomes adoration— adoro te—I adore you.

VII POVERTY

Abraham was God's friend. He was poor; God made him rich. It is in the power of the Spirit that we worship God. He makes us rich; we give back to him the gifts he has given to us and we become poor. There is probably no phenomenon more tangible today than our embarrassment over affluence, whether we are a member of a family, a religious community or a diocese. We have been blessed by God and by our people, and in terms of monuments we are rich, we are visible. And because we are visible, we are vulnerable. The awkwardness, the embarrassment of this new phenomenon, has brought about a new consciousness of poverty, demanding a new understanding of the gospel. Poverty, because it is a Christian phenomenon, is a mystery, a charism, a grace. Undoubtedly we are more familiar with the Marxist concept of poverty today than we are with the Christian phenomenon. Perhaps as God used Cyrus of Persia to bring his people to the promised land, so will he use Marx to restore to us a forgotten value. I remember Mother Teresa saying that one of the reasons why she continues to travel, which is her greatest difficulty and her greatest sacrifice, is because she cannot let the

Marxists outdo her. She tries to be as faithful to the Lord as are the Marxists to their own cause.

Poverty is something very old, yet something quite new. The Christian value is forever new. If it is not new, then it is not of the gospel, for the gospel is always good, always new. Our struggle with poverty is a matter of new hermeneutics. The gospel will continue to require re-translation. One of our great frustrations is that the gospel cannot be finalized once and for all. Every generation tries to find a certain actualization of the gospel. How we would like to be able to say, "Now I pray," "Now I am poor." But our accomplishment in one decade is our poverty, our embarrassment in the next. We can never say that we have arrived. To say that, is to lose what we are. Poverty, or any Christian truth, has to be continually discerned and sought after. Poverty is the mustard seed which sinks its roots ever deeper within us. Subtly and suddenly, without our scarcely realizing it, the luxuries of our society became necessities. Only in our exposure to the Catholic world do we become aware of the gap between the gospel message and who we are.

The distinctiveness of Christian poverty lies not in reference to things but in its relatedness to people who are poor. Christ emptied himself so that he might identify himself with us. All of the Christian values are relational. They involve a certain presence to others; they are always centered on people. Poverty is not a thing in itself; it is an identification, a relationship to the total Body of Christ. Christ describes himself as the one who preached to the poor. And he preached not so much by his words as by his presence with and to them; in him, the Word became flesh. We easily confuse Christian preaching with the speaking of words and their meaning. Christian preaching has never had reference to words. It meant rather the kerygma as a lived witness. It is what we are, not what we say. Even today, how much confusion we create in the effort to communicate because we try to do it on the verbal level alone. Faith is enkindled and spread by the word incarnate. We must be the model, the medium.

We are poor today in almost a reverse way. We have so many things and who of us is not embarrassed by what we have. Our consciousness of poverty is different from that of the previous generation. Our poverty stems not so much from the absence of things as from the presence of things. It is a presence first of all to oneself, it is a presence to others, to the anawim, it is especially a presence to Jesus and to his Father. The Father emptied himself in giving us Jesus. Jesus emptied himself in coming to live in our midst.

Poverty is a sacrament in the sense that it reveals to us where we are; our poverty is a revelation event in our lives. It is the consequence of grace. It is not a virtue in the sense of a moral virtue which we work on from the outside. We become poor to the degree that we experience his presence in us, to the degree that things no longer have power over us. Poverty is a revelation of freedom which gradually takes over in us; he becomes our "enough." Poverty is more than some kind of strenuous violence done to ourselves. It is the peaceful growing within us of a new kind of freedom. Many years ago *Integrity* Magazine had a picture on the front cover of a Franciscan walking through a department store with a cherub smile on his face, utterly free of all the attachment which most of us experience when walking through at least a bookstore. "The birds of the air have no barn, but our heavenly Father feeds them day after day." Poverty is a relationship to the Father. It is an experience of providence. As Christians we are called to trust in the Lord. We do not believe that God will prevent evil from happening to us, rather we believe that even were we to be destroyed, we would still be called to trust in him. Should even the birds be frozen to death, still would we be called to believe in the Father. This is where faith comes in. We would not have to believe if he always saved us from our foolishness.

Not too many of us can claim to be poor with the poorness of Christ, the poverty which looks upon all things and says, "This nearly belonged to me, or could belong to

me if I chose it." We have been pro-
grammed for affluence, for comfort and
ease. I remember when I was in the desert,
how really luxurious it was because of the
quiet and the cleanliness. I did not realize
what a luxury it was to live in the desert
until I arrived in Recife where I stayed with
our two diocesan priests and five Immacu-
late Heart of Mary Sisters. There was never
a moment in which the radios of the
neighborhood were not playing from 4:30
in the morning until 2:30 the following
morning. There was no sanitation, no glass,
no screens on the windows; there was the
constant noise and an utter lack of hygienic
facilities. It took me four weeks to overcome the restlessness, the nuisance, the
vibrations which this caused in me. I
thought of the luxury of the desert, the
utter quiet and peace. I came to realize the
extent of my cultural impediments. It is
one thing to think missionary; it is another
to be there.

Poverty is a consequence of being in
Christ. Poverty is a radiation of love.
Poverty is relational as is every Christian
phenomenon, relational to his people and
to himself. It is a facet of charity. This is
what is so important to remember in
discernment. Poverty is not something
which exists by itself, rather it is related to
the ultimate charism of Christ which is
simply his love for all. In some way the
Marxists have us hands down when it
comes to poverty. Poverty has to be the

"dabar," the lived value. It is a truth; it is a gift to be received, not an achievement to be attained. Today there is a conversion to the struggle for liberation in politics, economics, and social life. This speaks to us and reminds us of a forgotten truth. Today there are new escapes from the old poverty. We are forever finding new escapes from the poverty of the gospel, new escapes from powerlessness. One of the temptations of our day is what I call "apostolic efficiency." You get the right heads together, we have the means and we will take care of it. It is similar to the old days when we had our big parish plants—God is in heaven, let him stay there and we will take care of the rest of it. Poverty, because it is personal and interior, therefore, is relative because all things in themselves are ambivalent, all things are good in themselves. There can be a conspicuous kind of poverty which is pharisaical. We each make our own unique kind of poverty. We each have a unique facet of poverty. Vatican II could not come up with a description let alone a definition of what poverty is to be for the Church because it is relative to each person.

Actual poverty remains the privileged path. The primary witnesses to the gospel are not the theologians, unless they also happen to be saints, which does not necessarily follow. We have not had too many affluent saints. If actual poverty is a privileged matter, it is also a chosen path. Poverty is one of the greatest expressions of Christian freedom. Unless it is chosen, it cannot be Christian. Poverty is a kind of sacrament which has to be discerned from within; it is the mystery of Christ always choosing poverty. He had no place to rest his head and no one on whom to rest his heart. Kirkegaard wrote about the meaning of "my." What does "my" mean? Does it mean that this is mine? Is it possessive? Or does "my" mean all that I have is yours. To what degree is all that I have yours? What is your most prized possession right now? It would be an interesting spiritual exercise to place your most prized possession on the altar some day. It is noticeable that as one grows in becoming poor, he becomes free to appreciate all good things. If we grasp something with our hand, we lose our hand. Things can destroy our freedom. The smallest thing is as capable of destroying our freedom as is the greatest thing.

Poverty opens us out to our brothers and sisters. One cannot be poor and isolated at the same time. One thing which struck me forcibly in South America was the fact that affluence afforded a quiet and a distance unknown to the poor. The richer one is, the further removed is he from people, the more privacy he enjoys. The poorer one is, the less privacy he experiences, the more crowded is his life. Perhaps one of our greatest luxuries are the walls and doors we take for granted. I recall Father Voillaume saying once that there were certain things that the poor possess which we do not have a right to; for example, a colored television. But there are things which the poor do not have which are necessities for us; for example, a hermitage, a place of quiet. A luxury for the poor becomes an imperative for us. This is where real discernment is necessary.

Simplicity and poverty: purity of life, single-mindedness; the celebration of things rather than the consumption of them; a quality rather than a quantity; one flower rather than a bouquet. Poverty is consecration. Perhaps in our society which is marked by over-choice and over-experience, one of the greatest impediments to a life of deeper prayer is the plethora of things and possibilities. Rome is a good experience because of the over-choice. There are so many places to go, so many things to see, and there is the desire to do everything all at once. Never before have we been so poor. There are so many things which I cannot do, so many places which open out before me and I cannot go to them. There is a deeper kind of poverty which is possible for us now than ever before. More people are destroyed by affluence than by poverty. More religious are lost through affluence than through uncelibacy.

What would it cost you most to part with? What is your litany of the poor? This is my litany: I am poor because I am a sinner; poor because I am in need; I am poor because of my unconversion, my unending repetition of failings and weaknesses; I am poor because of so little talent, so little energy, so little time; I am poor because I need so many people; I am poor because time moves faster than my feet, my hands, my heart. Who is your litany of the poor? How many poor people do you know? How many hours have you spent with people who are literally poor? When Charles de Foucauld's confessor gave spiritual direction, he demanded that each of his penitents spend at least an hour a week with a poor person. How has he led me to be poor? How does his presence free me to be poor? How is poverty a beatitude in my life? What have been its effects upon me?

VIII CELIBACY, THE NEW FRONTIER IN HUMAN SEXUALITY

Celibacy has a strong and deep parallel to prayer, for both are a presence to oneself, a presence to him, a presence to others. Celibacy is Christian only if it is a sign of his presence within, a presence which frees one from oneself for him and for others. Celibacy in, with and through Christ carries with it a new depth of adoration and thanksgiving toward not only his presence in himself but toward his presence in others. Celibacy is the depth prayer of the body. A new grace begins to grow, a springtime in autumn. I come into your presence with flowers, to light candles and burn incense. I come to venerate. I feel like the earth when it is in bloom and fruitful. I will not take to myself what I could. I will eat my hunger and drink my thirst as the Master did before me and his disciples ever since. The one who is celibate in Christ loves beyond what is seen or possessible. He or she loves the hidden self which is yet to be revealed. How we are changed by the cumulative hallowed presence of another in us! How we create others by loving them beyond what they have ever experienced or imagined!

Celibacy is a sign of the resurrection, of the Spirit's presence activating the resurrection now. Christ came to redeem man by restoring him to his original integrity and innocence and the sign that man is restored is his reconquest of chastity. Celibacy no less than Christian marriage is the sacrament of sexuality, the sacrament of the sacredness of the life power and life sources. It too affirms the sacrament of touch, of embrace and kiss consecrated to him. There is a unique depth in a person which comes out of fidelity, a depth which grows endlessly because he says "no" to all except the one and only, to whom he says "yes" with all of his being and love. This becomes possible only when "we ourselves have known and put our faith in God's love toward ourselves" (1 John 4.16), which in turn becomes creative, all inclusive and overflowing to others: "I call you friends because I have made known to you, everything I have learned from my Father" (John 15.15). Celibacy is one of the most tangible and visible expressions of the ongoing Paschal Mystery. "A man can have no greater love than to lay down his life for his friends" (John 15.13), and for their sake I consecrate myself so that they too may be consecrated in truth. Each day the priest-disciple of Jesus renews his covenant with him, "This is *my* body given for you; this is *my* blood to be shed for you for the remission of sin."

Elie Wiesel, a contemporary writer whom I enjoy immensely does not write of love, friendship or celibacy but he does write about the ground out of which they come—God, man alone, suffering and prayer. "But to say, 'What is God? What is the world? What is my Friend?' is to say that I have someone to talk to, someone to ask a direction. of. The depth, the meaning, the very salt of man is his constant desire to ask the question ever deeper within himself, to feel ever more intimately the existence of an unknowable answer." Wiesel comes back to this theme again and again. "Who says that the essential question has an answer? The essence of a man is to be a question, and the essence of the question is to be without answer." (*Town Beyond the Walls*) He explained to me with great insistence that "Every question possessed a power that did not lie in the answer. 'Man raises himself toward God by the questions he asks Him,' he was fond of repeating. 'That is the true dialogue. Man questions God and God answers. But we don't understand his answers. We can't understand them. Because they come from the depths of the soul, and they stay there until death. You will find the true answers, Eliezer, only within yourself!' 'And why do you pray, Moche, I asked him?' 'I pray to the God within me that he will give me the strength to ask him the right questions!' " (*Night*)

To ask the right question, to risk some kind of answer is the imperative laid upon the celibate priest today. G. K. Chesterton once said that anything worth doing is worth doing poorly. With that at my masthead, I begin my response. I write because the question is so persistent today. I write for my seminarians, for my priest and sister friends, for my lay friends. I write because too many have been silent for too long. I will write primarily of friendship and love, of relationship which I think is at the heart of celibacy. What I intend by the term "celibacy" is practically and in common sense usage synonymous with the vow and promise of virginity-chastity. Celibacy is not simply "non-marriage." It is a positive and wholehearted commitment to Christ. Celibacy is more than a means to an end. I find it hard to conceive that any Christian would choose non-marriage as a difficult means for the achievement of an evangelical project, having no more importance than to help one achieve that end. If there were such a celibacy (which I seriously reject), a celibacy no more important than any other optional means to the evangelical project, then it would logically follow that "should it become evident to him or her either that he cannot continue to pursue the goal, or that celibacy is no longer conducive to that goal, it makes sense to abandon the celibacy." Celibacy is not a means to an end but rather a relationship of discipleship.

History continues to reveal a cumulative affinity and an inner congruity between celibacy and priesthood. It can be a yoke and burden and will become so unless one knows him and hears his words: "my yoke is easy and my burden light." "Come to me all you who labor and are burdened and I will refresh you."

This very recent theological distinction of celibacy as non-marriage, extrinsically dictated and never-inwardly chosen, I think, is untrue to tradition and unfair especially to the tradition of the diocesan priesthood. Celibacy is not born fully matured, no more than any marriage reaches the heights of fidelity on the wedding day. Fidelity evolves and grows as marriage and celibacy unfold, beginning with outer norms and moral imperatives which are but gradually understood, wrestled with and intrinsically chosen. Many may fail to assimilate the intrinsic meaning of marriage or celibacy, but failure does not invalidate the reality or demand that the substance be changed. In our modern age we have witnessed a development of the human consciousness evolving into a recognition of the importance of human choice. Man has gradually come to be more present to himself. He has become increasingly aware of himself as a subject for whom to live means to determine his life by his own free decisions placed in response to the affirmation he personally has made about what is true or false, what is good or evil. That way of thinking which finds the basis of order mainly in the world outside of man is giving way to the affirmation that order is more basically founded in man as subject. Man consciously becomes the foundation of human meaning insofar as the direction of the forces of this world, especially man himself, are dependent upon personal judgments of truth and value and upon consequent free decisions. This is why the focus and burden is so much more on the person than on the institution.

The priest in every era has a gauntlet to run, some equivalent to the walking on water. Perhaps for the priest in our day it is celibacy. "Jesus called out to them, saying, 'Courage! It is I! Do not be afraid.' " It was Peter who answered, 'Lord,' he said, 'if it is you, tell me to come to you across the water.' 'Come' said Jesus. Then Peter got out of the boat and started walking toward Jesus across the water, but as soon as he felt the force of the wind, he took fright and began to sink. 'Lord! Save me!' he cried. *Jesus put out his hand at once and held him.* 'Man of little faith,' he said, 'why did you doubt?' " "What you have hidden from the learned and the clever you have revealed to the merest children" (Luke *10*.22). "And so he can sympathize with those who are ignorant or uncertain because he too lives in the limitation of weakness. That is why he has to make sin offerings for himself as well as for the people" (Hebrews *5*.2).

Celibacy evolved in the priesthood not out of prescription, of law and discipline, but out of experience, of choice, of the disciples' existential inability to be otherwise. Celibacy was a description of the priesthood, a lived experience of a faith response. It was never an end or goal itself but simply a concomitant, a consequence of discipleship, like the thread of a needle. Celibacy never subsisted in itself and has no faith meaning in isolation. It drew its life and meaning from a vision and subsequent cluster of interlocking values. Celibacy is a value which takes its life and spirit from the faith-vision of Jesus himself. When that faith-vision is dimmed or displaced, the secondary values become unintelligible. Then the disciples' tradition embedded in a law loses its prophetic power and promise and has to be rediscovered all over again.

A new "anthropological" model of the priest is complementing the older "theological" model, and this development is good and necessary because all theological systems are time-limited and culture-bound. The birth of deeper truth is painful and traumatic, ripping and sundering. New perception comes at high cost and some values are dimmed and lost in the transition.

The "model" transition of the priest broke upon us at the high tide of existential personalism, with its new depth of interpersonal relations, and the all encompassing and absorbing revolution of marriage and sexuality. Now as the tide goes out and enthusiasms cool, one can begin to look at what happened and what continues to evolve.

Celibacy for most priests was simply there, like shaving every morning. You never thought it could be otherwise. I do not remember a serious discussion on celibacy before the mid-sixties. There was no special preparation for celibacy, any more than there was preparation for marriage in our universities. It was not perceived as a major factor or problem in a priest's life. It was the grand assumption and valid for the most part thus far, that each priest would grow into his celibacy as his brother would grow into his marriage. And in general it seemed that most were as successful or unsuccessful as their confreres in marriage. To be married or to be celibate did not seem to be the ultimate determinant in the unfolding of a person's life, happiness and holiness.

In the fifties, we took it for granted that all of us were loving and lovable and that the easiest thing in the world would be to get married as does the other 98% of the population. We thought that if one were not capable of being an excellent husband and father one would probably make a poor priest. Our contemporary experience has validated both points. Not to get married meant acting against the ever present current, the marriage gravitation pull. It meant a personal discipline and esprit de corps. We were to be to other women as a married man is to other women. We did not play the dating, the courtship game. Each man tried to know his own perimeter, to draw the line which he had to draw, to learn what was appropriate and not appropriate for him. Perhaps we overpresumed on the grace of the Lord, but we felt secure in the heritage of all the priests who had gone before us.

One's relationship to God makes possible one's celibacy. Celibacy is a "state of life" kind of word, a word impersonal, clinical, faceless, factual. Caelebs means alone, unmarried. But it is not a static concept; it doesn't simply happen, it is not a simple negation, taking place by default. It is an adventure, an achievement, a search and pilgrimage as much as marriage is. It is a path to be walked, a mountain to be climbed. It is not the convex of the concave, nor the negative share of the frame, gestalt. The possibilities in each human person are so much richer than we dare imagine. Remember Frost's poem about the fork in the road, "I chose the less traveled one and it made all the difference." "And it made all the difference." Too many, too soon and too easily surrender to the behaviorism and sociologism of contemporary mandatory marriage. Modern sociology and psychology have demonstrated the power of the negative self-fulfillment prophecy. If the whole society "hexes" you, telling you you cannot achieve, you will believe the society's hex.

The sociology of knowledge, the network of unrecognized societal presumptions and values, the subliminal influences, all the more powerful because unconscious, can even offset one's conscious faith values and mute the action of the Spirit. But there is also a positive prophetic self-fulfillment. Faith, Hope and Love are prophetic self-fulfillment acts. Every command of Christ is a prophecy, a power, a promise. His life is an invitation, his call to come and see, come and follow, are prophecies over ourselves. Faith, hope and love release tremendous energies within us that the world has never seen before, the power of Christ loving in us. He alone makes the impossible possible, and not only for the extraordinarily gifted human persons but for the likes of us, littles ones and poor. "We are only the earthenware jars that hold this treasure, to make it clear that such an overwhelming power comes from God and not from us. We are in difficulties on all sides, but never cornered; we see no answer to our problems, but never despair;. . .always, wherever we may be, we carry with us in our body the death of Jesus, so that the life of Jesus, too, may always be seen in our body. Indeed, while we are still alive, we are consigned to our death every day, for the sake of Jesus, so that in our mortal flesh the life of Jesus, too, may be openly shown. So death is at work in us, but life in you" (2 Corinthians *4*.7). And again, Paul writing to the same "anawim" of Corinth, the marginal rejects of that society, says: "No, it was to shame the wise that God chose what is foolish by human reckoning, and to shame what is strong that he chose what is weak by human reckoning; those whom the world thinks common and contemptible are the ones that God has chosen—those who are nothing at all to show up those who are everything. The human race has nothing to boast about to God, but you, God has made members of Christ Jesus and by God's doing he has become our *wisdom,* and our *courage,* and our *holiness* and our *freedom.* As Scripture says, 'if anyone wants to boast, let him boast about the Lord.' " (1 Corinthians 2.27). We seldom do more than we have to. Biological and psychological imperatives inculcated by a particular culture repress the deeper freedom of many. In such a leveling and unimaginative society, differences are suspect and threatening. Celibacy becomes an annoying and embarrassing intrusion.

Celibacy is in the crucible. It is good that it is there. It needs refining and purification. Demythology and depedestaling is the penalty it must pay for those who pushed it to idolatry. But it will emerge stronger and deeper than it has ever been before. Perhaps it has never been so needed as it is today. Celibacy is not a diminishment of man/woman but an intensification of the human person. Celibacy is on the cutting and growing edge of man transcending himself. As Rilke expressed seventy years ago: "Love will no longer be the intercourse of man with woman, but that of one humanity with another. And this more human love (this love full of respect and silence, sound and sure in all that it binds and looses) is indeed that for which, in strife and pain, we made ready; it consists in this, that two solitudes protect, limit and honor each other." This will be the meaning of fully developed people as persons, a type of relationship into which people enter as persons with the whole of themselves. There will be space and freedom for growth in which each person will be the means of releasing the other. Rilke maintains that "a complete sharing between two people is an impossibility. . .once the realization is accepted that even between the closest human beings, infinite distances continue to exist, a wonderful side by side can grow up, if they succeed in loving the distance between them which makes it possible for each to see the other whole and against a wide sky."

Each of us has an almost unlimited scope for personal development. Some studies indicate that most leave ninety percent of their potential unused and untapped. A man, a woman will develop and grow in one way if married; then will grow in a different way if celibate. Both are possible, both are valid, both are healthy but no one person can have both. Both ways will make a fundamental difference in the unfolding of one's person and personality. Ivan Illich writes that sexual renunciation does not make prayer more intimate, love more ardent, or graces received more abundant. A priest seeks no abstract or concrete reason for his decision. Efficiency corrupts Christian testimony more subtly than power. His choice is a pure risk of faith, the result of the intimate and mysterious experience of his heart. He chooses to live now the absolute poverty every Christian hopes to experience at the hour of death. His life does not prove God's transcendence, rather his whole being expresses faith in it. His decision to renounce a spouse is as intimate and incommunicable as another's decision to prefer his spouse over all others.

How does one know if one has the capacity for celibacy? How long does it take? How many years does it take to become a lover? a husband? a wife? a friend? How long does it take to become your own person? Is it a matter of making a decision and *seeing to it* that it is the right one? Is it, as it is in marriage, you know you must go all the way or you won't make it? In the old structures and social conventions an outward celibacy simply happened. There were few opportunities or possibilities to be otherwise. You were innocent, not virtuous. You did not earn the psalm and blessing of the man who could have sinned but did not. That outer celibacy was dangerous because it created the illusion that you were celibate inwardly. It is no wonder there was a crisis when the social and cultural conventions disappeared. Celibacy did not fail; it simply had not been found. Sexual segregation of celibates had set unacceptable limits to virtue and had accepted as a norm the immaturity of some dedicated persons. Yet holiness is certainly beyond people who cannot be chaste in the normal course of human relationships, whose chastity depends on cloister rather than virtue. There is today a new world of interpersonal relationships, a new frontier in friendships between men and women. Consequently a new inner depth of celibacy is being discovered and developed. It is a new phenomenon, a new growth of the old mustard seed.

What is it that prepares for friendship, love, celibacy? Surely it begins with the warmth and expansiveness of one's own father and mother, brothers and sisters. Their range of affection and friendship is the seed of one's own. The friendship of late adolescence, the cor ad cor loquitur, when one discovers the depth and range of the human heart and spirit, that one is not alone in the world, that there is a "you, too!" who shares the uniqueness of one's life, the sharing of mind and heart, dream and fantasy, hope and fears. "O sweet mystery of life at last I've found you." Every popular tune expresses a richness which it never had before. One sees a mystery of truth and beauty which is invisible to the rest of the world. Men friends prepare the way for women friends. One intuitively understands that life is most of all the friends you have made. Deeper and more personal levels are discovered and developed. Your friend's friends become more his friends because they are your friends. No professional person is given the depth and breadth of friendship which is given the young priest. All that could possibly be given to Jesus Christ is given to him. He cannot help but enjoy and "in joy" being "Father" being "Jesus," not in any pride, but in profound humbleness and reverence. Like the "Little Prince" and his rose, his people become unique in all the world. He is responsible for the people he has "tamed" and they become responsible for him. He and they are important because of "the time they have wasted with each other."

Every friend enriches one's capacity for friendship and enriches all previous friendships. One's capacity is stretched until he wonders how many can fit around his table,—twelve—thirty-six—fifty-two—one for every week of the year?—seventy-two? He has given us his spirit as the *first* gift to those who believe, the second? third? are undoubtedly all the other friends he sends into our life—30, 60, 100-fold in this life and then life everlasting. We have the capacity for God, therefore we have the capacity in someway for the four billion other persons who breathe this planet's air with us.

This is the enthusiasm of a priest's first few years, or at least it used to be. His life is made up of those whom he loves and who love him. Then suddenly, unexpectedly the noon day devil appears but always as an angel of light, a new unfolding of the spirit. Entrophy and amnesia have already prepared the way. Nothing dramatic takes place. "Filled with the Holy Spirit, Jesus left the Jordan and was led by the Spirit through the wilderness, being tempted there by the devil for forty days." It is not quite as neat and classical as that. It is closer to Mark's description of "the Spirit *drove* him out into the wilderness. . .He was with *wild beasts* and the angels looked after him." And the forty days are more akin to the Israelites forty *years.* Carl Jung in his *Man and His Symbols* writes deeply of this kind of desert. "Man feels himself isolated in the cosmos, because he is no longer involved in nature and has lost his emotional "unconscious identity with natural phenomena, his mystical participation". . .No voices now speak to man from stones, plants, and animals, nor does he speak to them believing they can hear. His contact with nature has gone and with it has gone the profound emotional energy that this symbolic connection supplied." And to sound out this insight, we have in our day Heisenberg's principle of indeterminancy shutting out the delusion that we can comprehend an absolute physical reality.

Some ancient spiritual writers held that the spiritual, reflective life began at thirty-three. Certainly a new spiritual combat lays hold of the middle years. Those who suffered through the many crises of faith of a few years ago now recognize them as initiations into faith. The stages of the new spiritual life are as significant as the mapping of the unconscious and the psychological stages of growth. Freud and all contemporary psychiatry has not progressed much in this area beyond Paul. "I cannot understand my own behavior. I fail to carry out the things I want to do, and I find myself doing the very things I hate. When I act against my own will, that means I have a self that acknowledges that the Law is good, and so the thing behaving in that way is not myself but sin living in me. The fact is, I know of nothing good living in me—living that is, in my unspiritual self—for though the will to do what is good is in me, the performance is not, with the result that instead of doing the good things I want to do, I carry out the sinful things I do not want. When I act against my will, then it is not my true self doing it, but sin which lives in me.

"In fact, this seems to be the rule, that every single time I want to be good it is something evil that comes to hand. In my inmost self I dearly love God's law, but I can see that my body follows a different law that battles against the law which my reason dictates. This is what makes me a prisoner of that law of sin which lives inside my body."

"What a wretched man I am! Who will rescue me from this body doomed to death? Thanks be to God through Jesus Christ our Lord! (Romans 7.15). One is compelled to recognize within oneself, the left hand as well as the right, the Dionysius as well as the Apollo, violence as well as reverence, the tendency to possess as well as to adore. One is confronted with violence to oneself at the risk of violence to another. Here I have found Jung's stages of the animus and anima helpful. The animus and anima in Jung's psychology are found in every person, man or woman. They are part of the preconscious movements within us that through experience and reflection are brought under discernment of spirits.

Stages of the animus
    wholly physical man—Tarzan
    romantic man—poet Shelley
    man of action—Hemingway
    bearer of the "word" political—
        Churchill, Kennedy
    wise guide to spiritual truth—Ghandi

Stages of the anima
    primitive woman—Eve, instinctive
        and biological
    romanticized beauty—Helen—romantic
        and aesthetic, still sexual elements
    love raised to heights of spiritual
        devotion—Mary
    sapientia—wisdom transcending even the
        most holy and pure Beatrice.

This is but a suggestion of the immense complexity contained within the vastness of our bodies and spirits, our earth and heaven, on the intersecting roads that lead us in the ways of human and divine love. To love is to enter into the secret of another, to experience from inside the mystery, depth, wonder, fear, intensity of another. To be "to" and "of" another is to experience "to be feeling for" and to reach the center of another in his totalness. Yet an anguished John Updyke can write "I remember lovemaking as an exploration of a sadness so deep people must go in pairs, one cannot go alone."

There is Spirit in the flesh and there is sexuality in the soul. Concupiscence, desire, curiosity, compulsion is there first and most immeditely and tangibly makes itself felt. The wound of human love is usually present long before the wound of divine love threads and edges the horizon. One is held by the Royal Gorge if one has no hint of Grand Canyon. The Spirit and soul are late comers, late developers. Their presence is not strong immediately, not sensibly felt, their hunger is much more quiet. The flesh would reduce all of the spirit to flesh, but the spirit, like mercury, is not that easily handled, not that easily reduced. The spirit overreaches itself in an attempt to sublimate the flesh into spirit. But the flesh is not so readily ignored or tamed. The flesh is good and holy for the Word became flesh. One was never intended to eliminate the other but both to be ordered and integrated into the whole person. There is an infinite hollowness and emptiness in the attempted fulfillment of one without the other; of the Spirit without the flesh; the flesh without the Spirit and it is in that moment that the other thunders most loudly, most deeply. It is folly to imagine that anyone can outrun the hound of heaven who is of earth. As we go along the way, we grow into him whom we are pursuing yet at the same time who is drawing us into himself. It is not so much we who make a journey to him, but rather he who is always coming to us. "When we finally see him face to face, we will recognize him as the one who was always with us."

We receive grace adequate to our development, our struggle, our temptation. We also seem to receive temptation in proportion to our grace! Temptation can be a call to recognize the grace which one has already received. Sin can be a revelation, a disclosure, an understanding, piercing and totally clear that this is not it! A terrible clarity, a sudden and ruthless obviousness that one is mistaken, in error, a fool! This is not what I was looking for—the utter transparency of the shock of truth!

"Of all things, be of love the most careful." Because love is the highest and deepest aspiration in the spirit of man, it is the most dangerous, most open to illusion, temptation and death. There is madness in every love, an untamed wilderness and desert of wild beasts. In times of twilight faith, a dark spirit of unlimited risk, an adventuresome fatalism tends to fill the vacuum of the soul. There are so many subtle paths of avoidance and escape from the restraint and discipline of faithful love. There is no mid-ground between love and hate, reverence and violence. Lovers too easily come to rage: "I hate you with all the violence of my love." Yet what is most deeply human is most deeply divine; where freedom is, there is grace, there love is. Love is abandonment. It is a terrible responsibility and beauty when someone gives us complete power over him or her self, the power and grace of a father before the innocence of his children, of a friend before a friend. Love forces one to the awesome awareness of the power one wields over himself and the power which is within. Love brings communion with persons almost in imitation of God's communion with them. The Father is in mystical union with every person whether they are aware of it or not and human friendship is always sharing in his friendship and communion with the other. There happens at times a certain illuminosity in deep graced friendships. One can almost discern the nimbus, the halo, the ring of love around each person and experience his presence through the infrared perception of the spirit and the heart.

Celibacy has not disappeared; it has not been fully discovered! I have thought often that even if celibacy had not been developed until our time, it would have had to have been discovered for the sake of man today. In 1914 Chardin prophetically commented that human development would plateau, be fixated and retrogress if man's sexuality were to be directed primarily by chemical and mechanical means. Christian celibacy, which is to say truly human celibacy, is becoming more significant for the development of man. It is a prophetic gift from Christ, latent and preserved in the Church, perhaps especially for our time. Celibacy is the unexplored frontier of human sexuality. It is the font of expansive and intensive friendship and love.

An adequate theology and anthropology of celibacy, love and friendship is but beginning. Perhaps we should begin with our early Church Fathers. Origen has much to say to us: Christ accomplishes his work of redemption of his fallen Bride by his progressive union with each individual Christian, a union that begins in the sonship established by baptism and develops toward perfect marital participation in the Body of Christ. Marriage and virginity are the two ways in which a Christian can experience the mystical marriage by way of participation. For Origen the superiority of virginity over marriage lies not in any moral comparison between two states, but in the comparative ontological status of the two realities. Marriage is an image of the heavenly marriage which is earthly and temporal, whereas virginity is a realization of the mystery in time which is not limited to time. Marriage has meaning only in this world; virginity begins in time yet will endure forever. Virginity is mutual self-giving between the soul and Christ. For Origen it is perfect freedom because it is perfect self actualization, the full realization of that for which he became Christian. It is not virginity which prepares for contemplation. But in contemplation, within which the soul receives the divine Word and conceives spiritually in the image of Mary, the person becomes truly virginal, truly Spouse of the Word. Celibacy is directed toward experiential union. The theology of virginity is an elaboration of the effect on the whole person when, by special grace, the mystical character of the Christian mystery becomes a personal experience. It is Christ's self gift to the soul with such experiential immediacy that it makes possible the total response of self gift in virginity.

Celibacy is an heroic situation. You cannot be heroic except in a heroic situation. Origen lived in a time when to be baptized was to be under a sentence of martyrdom. Origen's father was a martyr; it is possible that his son died the same way. Celibacy is part of that continuum of divine foolishness which is absurdity before the world—faith, martyrdom, celibacy, Christian marriage, fidelity. Celibacy like heroism is not grown into once and for all;

neither is faith or prayer. Each person will live a unique and personal faith, prayer, celibacy which will continue to unfold and grow with every experience of life.

Schillebeeckx has well expressed his rich insights into this Christian and therefore heroic situation in his book *Celibacy*: " 'We have left everything and followed you' (Matthew *19*:27). For them it was the inner logic of their enthusiastic discovery of the kingdom of God: 'for the sake of the kingdom of heaven.' In the synoptics the original experiential fact of this 'inner logic' is already formulated as a demand. Whoever wants to be Jesus' disciple must leave 'house or brothers or sisters or mother or father or children or lands' (Mark *10*:29–30; Matthew *19*:29). Luke leaves out 'or lands' but adds 'or wife.' Thus the meaning is to love God above everything. The suggestion that whoever belongs to Jesus' group in a special way cannot do other than leave everything and give up married life is an authentic biblical fact, in its essence independent of ancient ideas about man and his world. It can only be explained on the basis of the incalculable inner logic of a total surrender to the kingdom of God, next to which everything else pales by comparison. Jesus approvingly states a fact of religious psychology: in view of their joy on finding the hidden pearl (Mark *4*.11) some people cannot do other than live unmarried. This religious experience itself makes them unmarriageable actually incapable of marriage; their heart is where their treasure is. . .He who does not have this spontaneous experience, but voluntarily accepts the ministry and therefore clerical celibacy, devotes himself in full confidence in God's grace, through the acceptance of the celibacy law with special intensity to the kingdom of God. Thereby he at least gives evidence of his desire to enter in a special way into the realm of grace from which that celibacy intrinsically arises. This attitude is a call to God out of human weakness, to come under his spell in such a way that existentially celibacy becomes the only possible vocation. Personally I can experience my own priestly celibacy in no other way than in the form of continual beseeching, that existentially I may not be able to do otherwise."

IX THE PARISH PRIEST: PRIEST OF THE MULTITUDES

"What do you do?" "I am a priest." "Oh...!" Even today despite negative publicity, something of the aura of mystery rests upon the priest. Some respond with an excited, "Oh, that's wonderful!" Others respond with a look of anguished compassion. Most simply do not know what to say or how to respond. And their silence echoes back to me my own words, "I am a priest." There are times when I am startled by that assertion as well. Me...a priest! How did it happen? How does it continue to happen? From where did the desire come? How did the conviction take hold? How has it continued? How has it changed? Where does it go from here?

The question "why" is asked of the priest perhaps more than of any other person. There is question of a deeper level, an enigma, a mystery attached to a priest which is not attached to a doctor, a lawyer, engineer or teacher. There is something about a priest which touches the personal identity of each person. Whether we like it or not there is something "more" to this "vessel of clay." The priest is not just any man. He carries the prophetic Word and power, he is a prophetic act to the degree that he is poor, celibate and loving, that he suggests something more than this world.

The priest is "provocateur," he evokes love or hatred, welcome or rejection, peace or hostility. He is a sign of contradiction, of division. He comes with Good News, but he becomes bad news to those not ready. He comes to bring peace, but makes enemies instead.

A priest is someone else's man. He points to something beyond, deeper. He relativizes human absolutes. He calls or disturbs each man or woman stirring their heart of hearts. They have either to ignore him or to respond to him. Both take increased effort.

The priest is weak, is often a scandal. He is often not what he calls others to be. As a man he is no different than any other man. For the most part he is all too average.

A priest is a dependent, depending not only on Jesus Christ but on the Christian community. There is a reciprocal dependence, a reciprocal ministry. A priest is a reflector of Christ's priesthood or he can be a deflector. He is all too aware of the warning, "Be very careful what you teach them, they may learn it." The Gospel of one's life will penetrate deeper than the Gospel of one's words.

The priest is man on a journey. He is a pilgrim of the absolute. He is a God-hunting and a God-haunted man. He is a hound of heaven. He has been touched by the finger of God because he is a man called. Few men experience that call in a dramatic moment or all at once. Usually it comes as a slow dawning consciousness, like the dawning of reason or of age. One can only experience the conscious choosing of Christ and the slow life-long ratification of that choice, the beautiful experiences of being chosen by one's people, of being asked again and again in countless ways to be their priest, a second ordination, by one's people. In the process of being the instrument, the channel of his presence, something is deposited in the aqueduct. One becomes more and more confirmed in the mystery which is unfolded in one's life. One speaks and acts too often beyond one's talents and capacities for this is to be coincident or accident. His mysterious presence becomes more felt, sometimes like a brother's, other times like a stranger's, yet known. He seems at times to be one's twin, one's other self.

Something continues to happen in prayer, in the action of the Word. There is something of the magi in every priest. He is a sign watcher; he searches the heavens not only with his eyes but with his heart and soul. There is something in the soul of a priest which searches beyond into the twilight zones of man. His well is in the sky-heavens, more deeply than the astronomer, as constantly as the space-tracer. One would not gather it from the outside but each parish house, each Church is a tracking station, an exploration center, a space prober of God. Every priest is a pilgrim, a small star in the darkness wishing he could be the noon-day sun lighting up the whole land. Time, stars do not remove the darkness but you know they are there. They have light just enough for themselves and for those who seek guidance by them, like sanctuary lamps in the darkness.

As a pilgrim, the priest knows well his poorness of faith. There is no one who carries more doubts. Beside the doubts of all his people, he has his own to carry which are frequently even more deep, more agonizing. It is one thing to receive the Body and Blood of Christ consecrated by someone else. It is something else to receive Christ consecrated by your own words! It demands an even deeper existential faith. I shall never forget my first Mass. It was in the chapel over St. Peter's tomb in his Basilica in Rome. With not a little trembling, I uttered his words of consecration over the bread. I paused for an instant. *Nothing happened*! I was expecting something, anything—a peal of thunder, a quivering of the altar, but *something*! But nothing happened. Yet everything happened; he was there; he was present. Through my act of faith in his Word, he rendered himself present.

This ever silent dialogue of Faith is at the heart of a priest's life. How delicate, fragile is the stream of faith which must be the source of his faith for himself and for his people. A priest is preeminently a man not simply *of* mystery but *in* mystery.

Priesthood is the oldest specialized role of man, the highest, deepest, most mysterious profession. The Greek word for mystery most frequently designates religious rites which are always secret and hidden. No genealogy or heritage is older, none longer than that of the priest. The priest is a universal phenomenon in the history of man, from primitive man with his *shaman* and *mana* person to the historically recorded reference to "Melchizedek king of Salem (Jerusalem) brought bread and wine; he was a priest of God Most High (El Elyon). He pronounced this blessing: 'Blessed be Abram by God Most High, creator of heaven and earth, and blessed be God Most High for handing over your enemies to you. And Abram gave him a tithe of everything" (Genesis *14*:18).

The first Eucharist Prayer commemorates daily: "Look with favor on these offerings and accept them as once you accepted the gifts of your servant Abel, the sacrifice of Abraham, our father in faith, and the bread and wine offered by your priest Melchizedek."

In Egypt under Ramses III, around the time of Moses, ten percent of the population were priests! Imagine one priest to every ten or twelve people, like the Lord and his twelve! Eichrodt sums up the position of the priests in Israel as "the indispensable mediators for entrance into the sphere of the divine." They were the

custodians of the sacred traditions of cult
and of the knowledge of God.

Jesus applies the title "priest" neither to
himself nor to his disciples. But the idea of
a Christian priesthood is implicit in the
New Testament. The designation of priests
is first applied to the Christian community
in I Peter 2:5; Revelations 1:6; 5:10; 20:6.
These passages are all applications of the
title of Israel "a kingdom of priests"
(Exodus *19*:6) to the Church. The Church,
as the new Israel, fulfills also this character
of old Israel. The missing element is supplied in the Letter to the Hebrews which
deals almost entirely with the priesthood of
Jesus. Jesus was not a member of the tribe
of Levi; he could not be a "priest" in the
mind of a Jew. His priesthood is vindicated
by the application to him of the priesthood
of Melchizedek (Hebrews 7:1—17). Melchizedek as a man without father, mother
and genealogy is a type of the timeless Son
of God. He has a superior covenant, the
new covenant mentioned by Jeremiah 31,
the covenant which is a "testament" rendered effective by the death of the testator.
This death is sacrificially effective, for it is a
death by the shedding of blood (*9*:15—22).
As the priest, he has access to the sanctuary,
and he brings others in with him
(*4*:15—16). His priesthood is heavenly, not
earthly, which vindicates it against the
exclusive claims of Aaron. The dignity of
his priesthood rests ultimately upon his
sonship which is a far higher claim to

mediation and union with God than Aaron possessed. The ancient sacrificial cult, which was imperfect, is fulfilled in the sacrifice of Jesus (5:10); its atonement is perfect because of the excellence of the victim, himself. He has the solidarity with men which the priest as mediator must have. He has experienced human weakness, he has suffered, he is like his brothers in every respect, although he is himself sinless and therefore has no need of offering atonement for himself. He is the victim which he offers, not the animal victims of the old law. Therefore his one single offering need not be repeated and cannot be repeated, because it is totally offered, totally effective (7:27; 9:24–28). So the ancient sacrificial cult is abolished. The sacrifice of Christ effects redemption (9:12), salvation (10:18), forgiveness (9:15), purification (10:18), sanctification (10:10), perfection (10:14). It is the foundation of a new cult (9:14; 13:15 ff).

The priest is a cultic man, a ritual person. He is a dramatist, an actor, a liturgist, a man who is called to do public and sacred work on behalf of the community of which he is a part. We are not that far removed from the primitive Aymara Indians who project so much of their hopes into their rites that they actually come true. To be human is to be a symbol-maker. Christ and his disciples continued and created certain events, actions which held his presence, word and power and handed

them down to us through the Christian
community. We participate in these rites,
sacraments in such a way that we and
others draw a sense of direction for life and
encounter him who is always with us as the
way, the truth and the life.

Jesus assimilated all the ancient priesthoods within himself. He is all the priesthood which will ever be. There is nothing
of priesthood apart from Jesus. "There is
only one God and there is only one
mediator between God and mankind, himself a man, Christ Jesus, who sacrificed
himself as a ransom for them all" (I
Timothy 2:6). Christ was and is totally
priest: he filled to perfection the fullness of
priesthood. No one will ever be able to add
to his Priesthood. "No one takes this honor
on himself but each one is called by God as
Aaron was." Nor did Christ give himself the
glory of becoming high priest, but he had it
from the one who said to him, "You are
my son, today I have become your father,"
and in another text, "You are a priest of
the order of Melchizedek, and forever."
During his life on earth, he offered up
prayer, entreaty, *aloud and in silent tears*,
to the one who had the power to save him
from death, and he submitted so humbly
that his prayer was heard. Although he was
Son, he learnt to obey through suffering;
but having been made perfect, he became
for all who obey him the source of eternal

salvation and was acclaimed by God with the title of high priest of the order of Melchizedek" (Hebrews 5:4).

How much did the Eleven understand at the last Supper when he commanded them "Do this in memory of me," or even at the ascension when he said, "All authority in heaven and earth has been given to me. Go, therefore, and make disciples of all the nations." John would later contemplate and recreate these moments, "All that I have learned from the Father, I have made known to you, because of this you are my friends. . .as you sent me into the world, I have sent them into the world, and for their sake I consecrate myself so that they too may be consecrated in truth. I pray not only for these but for those also who through their words will believe in me" (Job *17*:18). What a consolation for the first priests, for all priests to follow in their footsteps. "I still have many things to say to you but they would be too much for you now. But when the Spirit of truth comes he will lead you to the complete truth. . .and he will tell you of the things to come" (Job *16*:12). A thousand years are as a day in God's eyes. Whether it be two days or two thousand years, we continue to wait and to be dependent upon that Spirit. It is difficult to tell by looking at a seed what shape the tree will take. It is even more difficult to look at the growing tree and imagine what the seed was like. The tongues of fire, the breath of the Spirit, reminding the Apostles that he would be with them always, launched them on their mission. They were faithful. No command entrusted to men has been more faithfully kept than his command, "Do this in memory of me." The development, the unfolding of priesthood will continue to the parousia. The apostles came to understand their priesthood through their lived experience. Each generation of priests, in their turn, pray, "May he give us the power through his Spirit for our hidden priesthood to grow strong" (Ephesians 3:16).

A priest carries or is burdened with a litany of titles and names, some from Scripture, some from history, all of them impressive, all of them personally awkward. Those names are not simply honorific; they are claims, cries of anguish, commands, prophecies. It is readily understood then why most priests desire anonymity. It is difficult to live up to the advanced billing of history, the unlimited expectations of people. The faithful, the people, have an intuitive sense for the sacred, for the holy person. Their faith in our *mana*, our power, is often greater than our own. They refuse to accept role-playing or the cultic-priest; there is always the humble prayer that we be what we do, that we become him whom we handle. This the greatest cross of a priest, the embarrassment of the distance between himself and the one whom he re-presences. Each person has his own unique way of asking the haunting question: "Are you the one who is to come, or must we wait for someone else?" (Luke 7:19). Every priest would like to cry out with John the Baptist, "No, I am not the Christ." "Well then, are you Elijah?" "I am not." "Are you the Prophet?" "No!" So they said "Who are you? What do you have to say about yourself?" What can one say? It is not enough to cry "I am a voice that cries in the wilderness, 'Make a straight way for the Lord.' " Who would dare? Paul's response, "Take me as your model, as I take Christ" (I Corinthians 11:1). "It was I who begot you in Christ Jesus by preaching the Good News. That is why I beg you to copy me!" (I Corinthians 4:15). It is somewhere between the Baptist and Paul that the priest finds himself. The description of Hebrews is more comfortable even though it is a description of the Old Testament priest, "He can sympathize with those who are ignorant or uncertain because he too lives in limitations of weakness. That is why he has to make sin offerings for himself as well as for the people" (Hebrews 5:2). The priest, to the degree that he knows the Holy, will also know sin. The more he knows Christ, the more he is aware of his own sin. "Here is a saying that you can rely on and nobody should doubt: that Christ Jesus came into the world to save sinners. *I myself am the greatest of them*; and if mercy has been shown to me, it is because Jesus Christ meant to make me the greatest evidence of his inexhaustible patience for all the other

177

people who would later have to trust in him to come to eternal life" (I Timothy *1*:15). The only request that Paul asks of his people is that they pray for him, "For fear that when I have preached to others I should myself be disqualified" (I Corinthians *9*:27).

"But I beg you, brothers, by our Lord Jesus Christ and the love of the Spirit, to help me through my dangers by praying to God for me" (Romans *15*:30).

"You must all join in the prayers for us, the more people there are asking for help for us, the more will be giving thanks when it is granted to us" (2 Corinthians *1*:11).

"Never get tired of staying awake to pray for all the saints; and pray for me to be given an opportunity to open my mouth and speak without fear and give out the mystery of the Gospel of which I am an ambassador in chains; pray that in proclaiming it I may speak as boldly as I ought to" (Ephesians *6*:18).

"Pray for especially asking God to show us opportunities for announcing the message and proclaiming the mystery of Christ" (Colossians *4*:3).

"Pray for us, my brothers" (I John *5*:25).

"Finally, brothers, pray for us; pray that the Lord's message may spread quickly, and be received with honor as it was among you; and pray that we may be preserved from the interference of bigoted and evil people" (I John *3*:1).

"Pray for us. I ask you very particularly to pray that I may come back to you all the sooner" (Hebrews *13*:19).

If Paul was such a beggar, such a collector of prayers, no priest can dare be otherwise. Sometimes our people forget how much we need their prayers. How often we forget how much we are sustained by the prayer and penance of those to whom we have been entrusted.

To be priest is to be identified with Christ and therefore to be a victim, unpopular though that notion is today. The priest is to be a suffering servant, the Ebed Yahweh of Isaiah, "It makes me happy to suffer for you, as I am suffering now, and in my own body to do what I can to make all that has still to be undergone by Christ for the sake of his body, the Church" (Colossians *1*:24).

When someone is tempted Paul himself is on fire. Paul does not ask from others what he himself is not making an effort to practise. "Think of God's mercy, my brothers, and worship him, I beg you, in a way that is worthy of thinking beings, by offering your living bodies as a holy sacrifice, truly pleasing to God" (Romans *12*:1). The Priest is a corporate person; he carries a whole people within himself. He is solidarity with them. In Christ, he is a victim for them, a vicarious substitute; he lives, prays, works, does penance for many. To the degree that a priest enters into this tradition today, the more he will appear the fool, the clown. This tattered remnant will always be present in the Church through her saints, those saints of the confessional, the office, the men of infinite kindness and tenderness. Most of the people who come to the priest are ordinary people drawn by ordinary grace. They are the multitude upon whom Jesus had special compassion. "So as he stepped ashore he saw a large crowd; and he took pity on them and healed their sick" (Matthew *14*:14).

"I feel sorry for all these people; they have been with me for three days now and have nothing to eat. I do not want to send them off hungry, they might collapse on the way" (Matthew *15*:32).

"And he took pity on them because they were like sheep without a shepherd, and he set himself to teach them at some length" (Mark *6*:34).

We are too familiar with the multiplication of loaves; we miss the wonder, the astonishment of the experience. Jesus used divine power just to provide *bread*! That is truly amazing! Like the hidden miracle of Cana; wine then, and now bread, more than can be used. He did not receive bread and wine from the people; rather he *offered* it to them in abundance! And to his disciples he gave the command "give them something to eat yourselves" (Luke *9*:13). What he had done, they were to do in their turn. He did not ask them to build a temple, not even a synagogue. He did not separate them from the people, make them cultic priests. They were first of all his disciples filled with his Spirit. Far from being static priests, they were called to be missionary disciples creating a community of believers by preaching the good news, rendering him present in word and sacrament, healing all that separated people from God and from one another. His disciples were to have compassion upon the multitudes, upon the city as he did. "As he drew near and came in sight of the city he shed tears over it" (Luke *19*:42). "Jerusalem, Jerusalem. . . how often have I longed to gather your children, as a hen gathers her brood under her wings and you refused" (Luke *14*:34).

Jesus sent his priests into the midst of people as his Father had sent him. "As you send me into the world, I have sent them into the world, and for their sake I consecrate myself, so that they too may be consecrated in truth" (John *17*:18). To consecrate is to offer oneself in sacrifice for one's people. Jesus continued, "I pray not only for these, but for those also who through their words will believe in me. May they all be one. Father, may they be one in us, as you are in me and I am in you" (John *17*:20). How much easier it would have been to let each man go his own way, create his own path in following Jesus. Perhaps the most astonishing truth of the New Testament is that Jesus prayed that there "be only one flock," one vine, one body, that his followers were to love not only himself but one another, as he himself had loved them; that they were to be a family mutually interrelated, indwelling in each other as Father and Son! Each disciple was to reverence the other as a gift from and presence of the hidden and silent Christ, one's unknown self. Each person in the Church, every member of the body was to complete and build up the other.

This is the great work of the priest, to build up the body of Christ in love. The priest is animator, the human breath of the Body, the leaven of the multitude, the channel of chastity, love. It was as apostles, as men with a mission, that Jesus made his disciples priests. They were to announce the Beatitudes, be peace-makers, community builders, celebrating and cementing that union with him in the Breaking of the Bread. They were to be as he was "Here I am I among you as one who serves" (Luke 22:27). "If I then, the Lord and Master have washed your feet you should wash each other's feet. I have given you an example so that you may copy what I have done to you." "I tell you most solemnly, no servant is greater than his master; no messenger is greater than the man who sent him" (John 13:14).

The priesthood in its most fundamental and universal expression is found in the parish priest. He is the priest of the multitudes who calls forth all the possibilities of his priesthood. The correlative of "priest" is "people." It is for them that he is ordained, consecrated. A man cannot be ordained for himself, for his own sanctification. He is called by the people of God from among men and is appointed to act for men in their relationship with God. "And so he can sympathize with those who are ignorant or uncertain because he too lives in the limitations of weakness. That is why he has to make sin offerings for himself as well as for the people" (Hebrews 5:1). Christ is the fullness of all the ancient priesthoods. His disciple-apostles continue that fullness of priesthood, but that is only a part of their total ministry as it was of Jesus'. The culmination of Jesus' priesthood and therefore of every priesthood, is to lay down one's life, to be the victim of one's own priestly act. "The Father loves me, because I lay down my life in order to take it up again. No one takes it from me; I lay it down of my own free will, and as it is in my power to lay it down, so it is in my power to take it up again; and this is the command I have been given by my Father" (John *10:*17). The great liturgical actions of the priest are the symbols, the remembrance and anticipation, the call and promise, of what he is called to be for the rest of the day. What is crucial is that the priest is not defined by his work, rather he specifies and stamps the work with his priestly character. Just as the Church is sign or sacrament to all men by representing Christ and his message, so too, the priest is a clear specific sign of the mission of the Church both to believers and non-believers. If everyone is a sign in the same way, then no one is a sign; for a sign, by its very nature, stands out from other things, draws attention in order to refer to something beyond itself.

Often times, like leaven, the priest seems to be swallowed by the people and he finds himself wishing he had a boat ready like Jesus. "And he asked his disciples to have a boat ready for him because of the crowd, to keep him from being crushed. For he had cured so many that all who were afflicted in any way were crowding forward to touch him" (Mark *3*:9).

The priest's power for the sacramental Body of Christ gives him his responsibility for the mystical Body of Christ, the people of God. This is the source of his call to holiness. To ask if the priesthood is a "state of perfection" is a non-question. It is enough to say that one is priest. He has to be like Christ. "Let this mind be in you which was also in Christ Jesus" (Philippians *2*:5). Of ourselves this is impossible. "Without me, you can do nothing." No one is more aware of this truth than the priest. Into the hands of a priest are given not only the Word of God and the sacraments, but the faithful themselves. The great work of the parish priest is the care of souls, of people. He is shepherd of a flock, pastor of a people. The greatest tribute his people can give to him is the faith-inspired title of

"Father." This is not an arrogant "clerical culture" word, rather it is a call and prophecy of the Christian people that the priest engender in them the sonship which he receives from the Father through Christ. The Faithful seem to have a deeper sense of the depth of this mystery, this "mana" Spirit power of the priest than he does himself. Paul writes, "You might have thousands of guardians in Christ, but not more than one father and it was I who begot you in Christ Jesus by preaching the Good News. That is why I beg you to copy me" (I Corinthians 4:15).

> "You are yourselves our letter, written in our hearts, that anyone can see and read, and it is plain that you are a letter from Christ, drawn up by us, and written not with ink but with the Spirit of the living God, not on stone tablets but on the tablets of your living hearts" (II Corinthians 3:2,3).

> "I must go through the pain of giving birth to you all over again, until Christ is formed in you. I wish I were with you now so that I could know exactly what to say, as it is, I have no idea what to do for the best" (Galatians 4:19).

> "We have spoken to you very frankly; our mind has been opened in front of you. . .I speak as if to children of mine, as a fair exchange, open your minds in the same way" (II Corinthians 6:11).

> "Like a mother feeding and looking after her own children, we felt so devoted and protec-

tive toward you and had come to love you so much, that we were eager to hand over to you not only the Good News but our whole lives as well" (I Thessalonians *2*:8).

"It is you I want, not your possessions. Children are not expected to save up for their parents, but parents for children. I am perfectly willing to spend what I have, and to be expended, in the interests of your souls. Because I love you more, must I be loved the less?" (II Corinthians *12*:15)

"I have made myself a slave of everyone so as to win as many as I could. . .For the weak I made myself weak. I made myself all things to all men in order to save some at any cost. . .(I Corinthians *9*:23).

"What I want to say now is no pretense. I say it in union with Christ—it is the truth—my conscience in union with the Holy Spirit assures me of it too. What I want to say is this: my sorrow is so great, my mental anguish so endless, I would willingly be condemned and be cut off from Christ if it would keep my brothers of Israel, my own flesh and blood" (Romans *9*).

"Keep a place for us in your hearts. . .you are in our hearts—together we live or together we die. I have the greatest confidence in you, and I am so proud of you that in all our trouble I am filled with consolation and my joy is overflowing" (II Corinthians *7*:2).

Although the priest is shepherd of a flock, pastor of a people, father of a family, he "lives with the rest of men as with brothers" (Vatican II). In St. Augustine's words, "For you I am shepherd, with you I am a brother." As a pilgrim, the priest walks with his people drawn by the Spirit of our common Father. The priest's ministry is a mutual enrichment; as he gives to each person he receives much in return. The priest continues to grow and develop through the people who call him to minister Christ to them. At times the priest ministers by letting people experience how much they mediate Christ to him. "If we live by the truth and in love, we shall grow in all ways into Christ, who is the head, by whom the whole body is fitted and joined together, every joint adding its own strength, for each separate part to work according to its function. So the body grows until it has built itself up, in love" (Ephesians 4:15). "For I am longing to see you either to strengthen you by sharing a spiritual gift with you, or what is better, to find encouragement among you from our common faith" (Romans 1:11).

A diocese is a place and a people. A diocesan priest is a man committed to a place and a people. For him there is a special permanence of place and time, a deep rootedness of history and tradition, an anchored stability in ever moving waters, a built-in Gibraltar-ness which stands between oceans ever changing and breaking. A Parish priest has no other community than his people. They are his primary relationship, like a father to his children, the Divine Shepherd to his sheep.

As a priest he is ordained directly, immediately to and for his people. They are his life-long trust. A priest says to his people, "I am your priest, you are my people. As a priest, I have no other family but you." A priest's fatherhood is in Christ. By not marrying he leaves open a vast unoccupied space in his heart which Christ and his people must fill; otherwise someone else or lesser things will fill him. The priest leads a dangerous life. In no other walk of life can a man choose to do so much or so little. There is the risk of becoming closed in upon oneself, of beginning to do good and settling for "doing well." He can have as much community and fraternity or as little as he chooses. Marriage has many more immediate, inescapable demands written into it. The priest discovers the beauty and grandeur of solitude which most people do not discover until old age or early tragedy. He is continually meeting people at the deep points of their lives, at the depths of their anguish and sin, prayer and love. He is continually being hollowed out. Each day he goes to the mountain, the altar, as the great receiver of the Gift which he is to minister to his brothers and sisters. The Word of God cuts into him a little more deeply each time. His people scar him and give him their wounds for healing. The priesthood never ceases to be a radical religious experience. In rendering Christ present, the priest is to become the transparency of Christ.

The parish priest is the priest of the multitudes, the priest of the city. And he frequently feels like Andrew with the five loaves and the two fish "but what is that among so many?" Often all that he can do is to be there, to be present, simply letting people know that they are worth his life, that there is nothing else he would rather do than to be with them. One priest whom I revere deeply is Msgr. Clem Kern of Holy Trinity Parish, the downtown skid row parish. He gave me my pastoral training. I have talked often with him, more often watched him, listened to others talk about him. I write more out of his life and thoughts than I write of my own. Most pastoral work is hidden, unknown. There is little glamour or adventure to it. Whatever is needed, is to be done in the human way in which Jesus would have done it. We are quick to reject, quick to hold back. We are richly blessed but not to the point of giving everything back. It is not enough to be aware of the message; we must be the medium of returning it to those most in need. In every diocese there has to be a place of last resort, of no rejection. In every neighborhood, there must be such a person, a house of hospitality, a Francis of Assisi, a Jesus Person. Who other than the parish priest? Would that the poor, the stranger before every parish house knew that "Here there is no rejection." "Here they take people in." In our culture there is an unwritten principle by which everyone is judged, "If you do not succeed, there is something wrong with you." The person in need is always suspect, always guilty until the opposite is proven. St. Vincent de Paul used to say, "When we give bread, we should be on our knees." The rule at Clem Kern's parish house is, "Interrupt our dinner"—the person calling probably doesn't have a dinner. People know that we do not have the answers to their problems, but they want what we have—our hope. How many people have no institution or social agency to care for them—the border-line psychotic, the marginal drifter, the sole survivor of a family. It is for the priest to move out into the community to be present to his people. Not much is demanded, just the ordinary old-shoe Catholic priest who accepts interruptions as his life.

Another priest I much respect is Bill Sherzer of St. Mary of Redford Parish, at one time our largest parish, now undergoing transition. He shared his pastoral experience with me. The pastoral priest is the one who seeks his assignment in terms of the needs of a diocese. The priest is to do with his people what he does with bread and wine—make them signs of Christ's presence. He is to make persons living Sacraments, signs of Christ's fidelity and fulfillment to be with us all days unto end of time. The Christian is the presence of Christ in the world, through the Word and Eucharist becoming Christ. The Priest is the minister of the Christian Community. He makes Christ operable. The extent to which Christ and the Spirit are operable in Eucharist and Word is the responsibility of the priest. His work is to extend priesthood, to render Christ more and more present in his people and in the world. The priest is a living sacrament; he is to bring his people into becoming living Sacraments. The priest is a sign, an actuality of Christ present and active. The priest has to see himself as this kind of sign, the Christ-presence. And his people have to see him as this kind of priest. As Christ went to Cana, to Lazarus' wake, so the priest goes as sign of Christ's presence. The Sacraments are bearers of the Word, living signs through which the priest trys to facilitate the meeting of God and man. He brings his people, his community into the experience of God. The dignity of a vocation is directly related to the life which is served. He who serves the heart of the community, serves most deeply. The more essential the service, the greater its intrinsic dignity. The priest is essential to the life of the community. To remove the priest from the parish is to lose the community. How sad it is to hear the words, "I don't want to get over-involved in sacramental ministry," which is to say I do not want to get involved in the heart of ministry, the deepest presence and power of Christ!

The priest is the lode or seed crystal around whom the Church forms. He is the sacrament of Christ's presence to his people. He renders him present by Word, by Sacrament, by his own personal presence.

His life is to be a prophetic action even without words. He models what he calls his people to be. He is a disciple, sometimes led by the Spirit, other times driven by the Spirit. He tries to shape and plan his life from an innermost personal center who is Christ, his Lord. In a unique way he knows more deeply than anyone, "Without me, you can do nothing." He knows that he is merely the instrument of this one permanent High priest, Jesus Christ, to whom "I bend my neck as victim to you who remains forever." As disciple of Jesus and therefore universal brother he is called to the unmapped mountains, desert and ocean of outer and inner space. He is a man of power, a power which is not his own and which could be self-destructive if used other than for Jesus and for his people.

LETTER TO A PRIEST

Calcutta
7 Feb. 1974

Dear Father. . . . . . .

You have said 'yes' to Jesus—and he has taken you at your word. The Word of God became man—Poor; your word to God became Jesus—poor. And so this terrible emptiness you experience. God cannot fill what is full—he can fill only emptiness— deep poverty—and your 'yes' is the beginning of being or becoming empty. It is not how much we really 'have' to give—but how empty we are—so that we can receive fully in our life and let him live his life in us. In you today—he wants to relive his complete submission to his Father—allow him to do so. Does not matter what you feel—as long as he feels all right in you.Take away your eyes from yourself and rejoice that you have nothing—that you are nothing—that you can do nothing. Give Jesus a big smile—each time your nothingness frightens you. This is the Poverty of Jesus. You and I must let him live in us and through us in the world. Cling to Our Lady—for she too—before she could become full of grace—full of Jesus—had to go through that darkness "How could this be done. . ." but the moment she said 'yes' she had need to go in haste and give Jesus to John and his family. Keep giving Jesus to your people not by words—but by your example—by your being in love with Jesus—by radiating his Holiness and spreading his fragrance of love everywhere you go. Just keep the joy of Jesus as your strength—Be happy and at peace—Accept whatever he gives—and give whatever he takes with a big smile. You belong to him—tell him—I am yours—and if you cut me to pieces every single piece will be only all Yours. Let Jesus be the Victim and the Priest in you. I have started going to visit our houses in India—so I have beautiful time along with Jesus in the train.

Pray for me as I do for you.

Yours in Jesus,

M. Teresa, M.C.

X WHATEVER HAPPENED
TO THE CHURCH?

Whatever happened to the Church?
Whatever happened to the Church who was
as familiar, as comforting to us as our own
home and at the same time called us to
expand our consciousness, connecting us
with millions of other parishes much like
our own throughout the world, through the
centuries. We did not pretend to understand all the mysteries our Church contained. That she possessed them and possessed us was enough. We simply rested in
the thought that we belonged to her.

"I belong to the Catholic Church."
Belong to—what an evocative word! What
an intimate word to describe connection
with the heavy abstraction "Catholic
Church." Every gathering of people has its
own language of intimacy. What may appear to be an abstraction to the outsider
may well be an intimacy to the one inside.
To *belong to* is to identify with, to be
identified by. It is with caution, hesitancy
that one identifies with anything today.
"I'm an independent," which is to say I am
not taking responsibility for anyone or
anything but myself. In our day, to say "I
am Christian," comes more naturally than
to say "I am Catholic." All Institutions, all

third person entities, "it," "they" are suspect. Only "you" and "I" are real; secondary relationships are nonexistential.

There is more to reality than that which enters our primary consciousness. To understand, to love the Church today, it is necessary to remember, to evoke our personal history and experience of "Church." What is our image of the Church? How do we describe her? Whom do we want her to be? Our expectation, our pain, our love for the Church results from our own ability or inability to reckon with, to appreciate the reality of sin and the glory of God in our own lives. The reality of our vision of the Church is dependent on the degree of our own spiritual maturity.

The Church is "the loving Mother of all." John XXIII. The Church *is* our Mother and we are her children. However, there is a difference in the mind-sets of the five-year old who clings to apron-strings for security and safety; of the adolescent who rebels for a confused vision of freedom and independence; and the adult who reverences the wisdom of experience, the endurance of years, the fragility of man, the constant journey into the fullness of Christ. The Church is our Mother and we ought not forget nor undermine the cumulative wisdom and Spirit vision which is hers; neither must we allow ourselves to ignore her human flesh and human blood in order to make of her a wishful fantasy to satisfy our needs and dreams.

Our experience of the Church gives an appreciation of the Spirit of Truth who fills her. The Church is not a classroom teacher. We cannot learn by rote or the mimicking of words, for her knowledge is not primarily of the lips or of the mind but is of the Spirit, of the essence of our lives. We come to know her Truth, she comes to know her Truth, by the co-mingling of our lives, the immersion, the integration of our lives into her life. We have responsibility toward the Truth of the Church, to deepen it, to discover it, to give it new expression. We are sent to bear fruit, fruit which will last, thirty, sixty, one hundred fold.

It is comforting, consoling to experience the Church as containing all Truth. It is disarming to recognize that she possesses only as much of this Truth as her pilgrim people have sought and found, asked for and received, knocked and had It opened unto them.

The old image of the Church was the mustard seed fully grown into the tree. The kingdom was well-established; it was simply a matter of time so we waited for the conversion of the world. There was simply nothing new to be discovered. The Church had already arrived in heaven.

To the Church of the forties and fifties, the Church in which I personally grew up, I owe a great gratitude. She saved me from myself, from anonymity, from the lonely crown. She bonded me to people, to the whole world; to the past in history and to the future in destiny. A corporate and communal identity was given to me. I became a part of a great people, an enormous history, an unshakeable destiny, future. The Church identified with and ingrafted me into Jesus Christ. The Church is Jesus Christ continued in time and history, the coming together of those who are called and sent by Jesus Christ to share him with others, the way, the truth, the life more abundant, knowing the only true God and him whom he has sent.

This was the stage of Church as Holy Mother, the unquestioned teacher and authority. She taught us to think, to stretch our minds over the ultimate questions, mysteries, but within definite restraining walls.

There was much security and comfort in that model of the Church. She was warm, intimate, personal. One came to know the city in terms of parishes. Where do you live? Or come from? was answered with the name of a parish. Actually the Church was my parish. It was human size, neighborhood-like, comfortable. This model of the Church as Mother, the primary image of Church, died sometime in the 1939-45 War. The formal notice was not fully publicized until twenty years later with the conclusion of Vatican II. The most far reaching decision of Vatican II was to decide whether the Church was to continue solely under the authority model or under freedom models. This was more a discernment of a reality which had already taken place rather than a decision taken. Pluralism of experience is the source and font of the pluralism of philosophy, theology, and is the cornerstone of new freedoms. Freedom is not clear and neat, well-ordered. Most often it is bewildering, confusing. Too many options and overchoice create either paralysis or polarity.

Today the Church is being taken very seriously. A great awakening has taken place. The Church is not a thing, some immoveable rock of Gibraltar. The Church is people; it is human; it admits of growth and decline, health and sickness, strength and weakness; it admits of being asleep or awake, dormant or alive. The Church is indeed the work of God and what God has brought together, no man can put asunder. The gates of hell will not prevail, but those same powers can give us a good "working over." The Church is also the work of man and man can play havoc with it. To be disappointed in the Church is to be disappointed in man, and if we just look at our own experience of ourselves we have reason to be disappointed. As Walt Kelly's Pogo said, "We have met the enemy and they is *us*."

We are disappointed in the Church because we expect her to be different from ourselves but she can only be who we are, or who we shall become. For we *are* the Church. The Church, born from the side of Christ, has been handed over, abandoned to men. She is the "pearl beyond all price" (Matthew *13*:46), purchased for us by his Blood, abandoned over to us in his Trust. The wild foolishness; the folly of Love! Christ himself is the worst offender of his own words, "Do not cast your pearls before swine" (Matthew 7:6).

The Church is ours, intimately ours; it has marched our history with us. We have walked her into sin, into scandal. We have left our skeletons in her closets, our scars upon her face. Still, she is ours, steadfastly, forever ours. We can be embarrassed by the Church, by her history, by her sin, by her scandalous fidelity to a humbled humanity. There will always be the Magdalenes, the Peters, the Charles de Foucalds for the Church to embrace. She will always be a scandal for she associates with sinners, sits at table, celebrates a meal with them. It is easier for us, though, to forgive the sin of the Church in the past, probably because it is the past; it is easier for us to forgive the sin of the repentant member simply because he is repentant. How difficult it is for us, however, not to become indignant at the corporate and present sinning of our Church. We know even through the experience of our own small world the scandal of the Church of the haves and the Church of the have-nots, the Church of the powerful and the Church of the powerless, the Church of the abundant and the Church of the starving, a starving unto death at times. What do you do with the Church of today?

Can we condemn her without recognizing that we are condemning ourselves? Do we use her as our scapegoat to avoid accepting our own personal responsibility for what she is and who she will become? Will we sit in her pews as an objective observer or will we see mirrored in her our own reflection?

The tragedy of the Church today is not that she contains sin; the tragedy is that we reject a sinning Church. We disaffiliate ourselves from her. "Many of his disciples remarked, 'This sort of talk is hard to endure! How can anyone take it seriously?' 'Does it shake your faith?' Jesus asked them. . .From this time on many of his disciples broke away and would not remain in his company any longer" (John 6:60–61,66).

The proof of the transcendent and immanent presence of God in the Church is not that she has never sinned but that she eternally survives her sin. If we are tempted at times to think that we are on a sinking ship we must remember that its Master walks on waters. The Church has been abandoned into our hands; if we are to survive the storm, we must abandon ourselves unto her, for in her destiny lies our own.

If the Church is of man, it is even more of God. Only the imaginative love of God could think of a Church. God has begun something *here*. He could not wait. The world to come has arrived; a beginning has been made. We have been invaded by extra-terrestrial life, by the Father, Son and Holy Spirit. There is a cumulative building of the communion of saints. The greatest witnesses to the Church are the saints, the happy, holy heroes and mystics. There is a cumulative wisdom, experience. The Church has its "arcana," its secret, its mystery of happiness, its fountain of youth. Its generativity is its saints. There is something *new* in the Church. It is you; it is me! There is something terribly alive in the Church, refreshing, quietly searching. There is a Second Spring; we are the buds. The Church is a plurality of experiences. We are the "underground Church" but also the Church of Silence. We are the Church of Evangelization and also the Church of the Poor, poor because we are members, at the same time rich because we are part of it. We are the Church of Rome displayed in magnificent splendor; we are the Church hidden in Japan without priests for 350 years. The most visible elements of the Church are not her most important, most essential ones. "Those parts of the body which have no obvious function are the more essential to health; and to those parts of the body which seem to us to be less deserving of notice we have to allow the highest honor of functions. The parts which do not look beautiful have a deeper beauty in the work they do, while the parts which look beautiful may not be at all essential to life! But God has harmonized the whole body by giving importance of function to the parts which lack apparent importance that the body should work together as a whole with all the members in sympathetic relationship with one another."

Damnation consists in having lost the sense of one's existence; it is the inexpressible suffering which comes when existence is devoid of meaning. "It is not good for man to be alone" (Genesis). Man is human only in and through a family. No man is an island, no man stands alone. "But God made things grow. Neither the planter nor the waterer matters, only God, who makes things grow. It is all one who does the planting and who does the watering, and each will duly be paid according to his share in the work. We are fellow workers with God; you are God's farm, God's building." "Everyone doing the building must work carefully..." (I Corinthians 3:9).

> "Just as each of our bodies has several parts and each part has a separate function, so all of us, in union with Christ form one body, and as parts of it we belong to each other" (Romans 12:6).

> "Together we are the body of Christ."

> "As every structure is aligned on him all grow into one only temple in the Lord, and you too in him, are being built into a house where God lives, in the Spirit" (Ephesians 2:22). "...and made him, as the ruler of everything, the head of the Church which is

his body, the fullness of him who fills the whole creation" (Ephesians *1*:22).

"He holds all things in unity. Now the Church is his body, he is its head" (Colossians *1*:17).

"If we live by the truth and in love, we shall grow in all ways into Christ, who is the head, by whom the whole body is fitted and joined together, every joint adding its own strength, for each separate part to work according to its function. So the body grows until it has built itself up in love" (Ephesians *4*:16).

". . .so that the saints together make a unity in the work of service building up the body of Christ. In this way we are all to come to unity in our faith and in our knowledge of the Son of God, until we become the perfect Man, fully mature with the fullness of Christ himself" (Ephesians *4*:12).

"You must speak the truth to one another, since we are all parts of one another" (Ephesians *2*:25).

Church means a togetherness of people who have found the Lord and continue to seek for him. The twentieth century has created a world consciousness, an earth awareness—space ship earth. Global war is the most tragic distinction of this century. It took man until this century to have the universal capacity to kill not only his brother Abel but the other half of the world. What international politics has not touched, economics and ecology have. The whole world, the whole earth has an awesome factualness about it today. Materially, physically, economically, ecologically, we are one world. The creation of the League of Nations, the United Nations, Unesco is the recognition by man, vague though it be, that for all his complexity, multiplicity, he is after all one, that he cannot insulate himself from himself, that he cannot survive independently or alone.

Never before have we so graphically understood that we are connected to one another, related to one another. We are forced to experience relationships with strangers, unknown, un-named who are continents away. We have impact, consequence on one another's lives. The physical separateness of space is no longer enough to stop our consciousness, our consciences from flowing into one another. Never before has there existed a greater need for a universal, catholic spirit; an expanded heart, a need to be universal brother and sister, not simply a cosmopolitan, a world citizen, but one committed, given for all mankind. Never have the words of St. Paul echoed more loudly in our hearts than they do today from all the myriad points on the globe: "Who does not stumble and I do not fall?"

> "For the weak I made myself weak. I made myself all things to all men in order to save some at any cost; and I still do this, for the sake of the gospel to have a share in its blessings" (I Corinthians 9:23).

"You should carry each other's troubles and fulfill the law of Christ. . .Everyone has his own burden to carry" (Galatians 6:2).

"I try to be helpful to everyone at all times, not anxious for my own advantage but for the advantage of everybody else" (I Corinthians 10:33).

"We who are strong have a duty to put up with the qualms of the weak without thinking of ourselves. Each of us should think of his neighbors and help them to become stronger Christians. Christ did not think of himself" (Romans 15:1).

"So let us adopt any custom that leads to peace and our mutual improvement; do not wreck God's work over a question of food" (Romans 14:19).

"Since you aspire to spiritual gifts, concentrate on those which will grow to benefit the community" (I Corinthians 14:12).

"Knowledge gives self-importance—it is love that makes the building grow" (I Corinthians 8:1).

"You must want love more than anything else" (I Corinthians 14:1).

Never have we had such insight into the world-wide, universal mission of the Church. Never before have we experienced her vulnerability and never before the need for the availability of her Love: Her Love alone has the power needed to achieve reconciliation, the force which is necessary to fuse us into one. The Church is the animator of the world, the center of its unity, because only of the Church can it be said, "This is God's dwelling among men" (Revelations *21*:3). From the concreteness of the Eucharist springs the eternal hope of the world. It is the tangibility of his Body, his Blood which compels us to believe his promise, his Word, to believe that his Church is at work in our lives even beyond our ability to comprehend it. "The mystery of the Church is not a mere object of theological knowledge; it is something to be lived, something that the faithful soul can have a kind of connatural experience of, even before arriving at a clear notion of it." Ecclesiam Suam.

To believe in the Eucharist is to believe that this "earth is passing away" and that he is, even now, making all things new. Who can measure the Spirit of God and the work he has already accomplished? We, as all youth, are impatient for completion. But if a thousand years is as one day in his sight, we are just two days young! The Eucharist does not simply give us the vision of what will be; the Eucharist Itself is the Global Force which causes this to happen. The Eucharist is the Axis about which we rotate, the Cosmic Pole to which we are magnetically pulled. Each day his Body, his Blood seeps deeper into the core of our earth. Each day his gravitational pull on our hearts, on our lives becomes greater. Each day the Church is more transformed, more transcendent. Each day she is more the New Jerusalem, the Holy City, coming down out of heaven from God. "The sacraments and the Church herself as the great sacrament are the place where the past, which is Christ as covenant and savior is present with a view to the future of the world through the action of the Holy Spirit." Congar.

The Church *is* the Body of Christ. Do we believe it enough? Can we ever experience it enough? I find myself increasingly caught by the mystery, the "holy ground" of every person I encounter. "Do you not realize you are temples of the Holy Spirit?" Each time the Bread is broken, distributed, we proclaim the Body of Christ. "The Body of Christ;" "The Body of Christ" and the words are echoed back from his people, "Amen, I am the Body of Christ." They come limping, smiling, poor, old, young, beautiful, "Amen. I am the Body of Christ."

The Church is the Church of the saints. Holiness is an adventure, essentially the only adventure, one of faith and love. Rites, creeds, organizations, traditions are necessary to protect and communicate life. They are the conditions of a social religion which give an individual history and destiny. Thanks to these conditions I participate in the faith of Francis Xavier, Thomas Aquinas, Augustine, Athanasius, and Paul. However, no rite exempts one from loving.

The Church bears her history, her burdens, her scars, her historic and human elements. She also bears the Divine; she is full of grace, the grace of holiness which comes entirely from Jesus operating in the innermost parts of man. She is the spouse of Jesus Christ and as such can claim to be our Spiritual Mother. Her profound life flows entirely from him. We will understand her to the degree that we seek to know him more fully, "Jesus is the only priest, the great celebrant of the world. He is in his offered body the only temple" (John 2:18–22) into which we must enter to live." "He cannot have God for his Father who does not have the Church for his mother." St. Cyprian.

XI LETTER FROM ROME
OPENING OF THE HOLY YEAR DOOR

Christmas Eve, 1974, 10:00 p.m.
St. Peter's Basilica, Rome

I was beginning my four hours of standing to take part in the opening of the Holy Year, the 1975 Jubilee Year. Never had I seen a crowd more packed or more alive. Momentarily I was literally lifted out of my shoes as I passed through one of the crowd barriers. I found a good position in the main aisle across from the famed statue of St. Peter and facing Bernini's Altar. As I stood my long vigil many thoughts and questions welled up within me. What was it that had drawn me there—to be in St. Peter's for the opening of the Door of the last quarter of the twentieth century? There are mysterious depths in each of us which we do not fully understand. There is a life within us which has come from milleniums before. Something within calls, moves us, and we do not fully understand, a homing instinct, a return to the place of one's birth, of one's ancestral heritage, of one's cultural origin. We are each on a "sacred journey," wanderers, wayfarers, pilgrims. The time of pilgrimage is but a more explicit consciousness of the inner journey. In the traditions of all of the great religions, pilgrimage takes the faithful back to the source and center of the religion itself, the place of meeting God, of conversion, of forgiveness, of holiness.

The spiritual history of our forefathers is no less alive in our veins than our biological heredity. The ancient roots of the spirit nourish us even when not seen or recognized. There is a oneness of Spirit, of Fatherhood, of Sonship which is too deep for consciousness to grasp. Yet there are privileged moments when intuition and grace grasp "something." I remember kneeling for the first time in the Pilgrims Chapel near the Basilica of St. Francis in Assisi. I experienced deep at-homeness and familiarity—something timeless—there where I had never been. There was but an unshakeable conviction and sense that "something" of me had been here before, back in the thirteenth century! It may have been wild imagination but it gave me a deep sense of bondedness to all those who had gone before and yet continued to nourish the great vine of which I am a bud.

Earlier that evening as I was walking to St. Peter's, I was thinking of all who have done the same thing down through the centuries, the "passing parade" in the "March of time." I remembered reading that in the year 1300 Dante visited Rome for the first jubilee and mentions in his poem that he saw the crowd of pilgrims passing in orderly fashion over one of the bridges of the Tiber to visit the Basilica of St. Peter:

> "...just as the Romans by reason of the great crowd the year of the Jubilee contrived a way for the people to pass over the bridge, so that on the one side all face toward the Castle and go to St. Peter's and on the other lane they go toward the Mount (Juniculum)." Inferno XVIII, 28—33.

The crowds are not so orderly today, especially at the entrances of the partitions and barriers which corridor off the Basilica. But as one comes into St. Peter Piazza and walks within the welcoming arms of Bernini's encircling colonnades one feels that one is in a sacred procession and is hushed with the cumulative reverence and prayer of the centuries. One is humbled in the presence of something so much greater than oneself, or one's lifetime. In the presence of twenty centuries one's life seems very small, yet very alive because I am a living member of all that is before me; it belongs to me and I to it, or rather they to me and I to them.

Back within the Basilica I was shifting my weight from foot to foot during the long wait before the ceremonies began and wondering why I did not think to bring a portable seat like some wiser people around me. My eyes roamed the grandeur of the Basilica and I remembered the expression of a young religious when she first entered St. Peter's, "Poor Jesus! Poor Jesus!," probably wondering aloud how the Gospel could have come to this. It does take one aback, especially today in our new sensitivity to poverty and simplicity. All those lights and color, those Cecil de Mille effects, the pomp and circumstance, the exhibitionism and flair for showmanship, the great dance and tableau of the splendor of Greece and the glory that was Rome's. All of this baroque was the work and play of the children of another age yet something of it echoes in all of us. It is irresistible in its own setting and incomparable. As students in Rome twenty years ago we had an adage, "See Rome and lose your faith; understand Rome and deepen your faith." Our Lord was not adverse to banquets or to a spectacular entrance into Jerusalem. He and his disciples were a scandal to their own times. "For John came, neither eating nor drinking and they say, 'He is possessed.' The Son of Man came, eating and drinking and they say, 'Look, a glutton and a drunkard, a friend of tax collectors and sinners.' Yet wisdom has been proved right by her actions" (Matthew *11*:18). And then again that strange passage of Jesus accepting the extravagance of Mary, the sister of Lazarus, "Then Judas Iscariot, one of his disciples, the man who was to betray him said, 'Why wasn't this ointment sold for three hundred denarii, and the money given to the poor?' He said this, not because he cared about the poor, but because he was a thief; he was in charge of the common fund and used to help himself to the contributions. So Jesus said, 'Leave her alone; she had to keep this scent for the day of my burial. You have the poor with you always, you will not always have me' " "You will not always have me," Christians have refused to let go of him. They, and we, continue to believe that he is with us! That faith in the Incarnate One in itself demands incarnate expression, to render visible what we believe in our hearts, to utter in some tangible way what the Spirit creates and erupts in us. St. Peter's Basilica is a symbol of a symbol, a symbol which is the sign of a sacrament. St. Peter's is a paradox, a symbol in reverse of the humbleness of Jesus and the simplicity of the Gospel. All of this grandeur exists to be the setting for a piece of bread and a cup of wine transformed into his Body and Blood!

St. Peter's is not a scandal. It is more a scandal that each Eucharist is not surrounded by a Basilica. The people of the Middle Ages followed a deep religious instinct when every town built themselves a Cathedral to celebrate the Body and Blood of Christ. Rome and St. Peter's are unforgetable because here is one place in the world where he is celebrated "as if they could see him." Perhaps in our culture we are developing a deeper Christian tradition: In place of building Basilicas, we are creating environments where each human person will be reverenced as a temple of the

Holy Spirit and will reverence themselves as more holy than the Cathedrals of old "and build one another up as living members of the Body of Christ."

> "Are you not worth much more than the birds in the sky" (Matthew 6:26).

> "Your body you know is the temple of the Holy Spirit, who is in you since you received him from God. You are not your own property: you have been bought and paid for. That is why you should use your body for the glory of God" (I Corinthians 6:19).

> "You have been bought and paid for; do not be slaves of other men" (I Corinthians 7:23).

> "Paul, Apollos, Cephas, the world, life and death, the present and the future, are all your servants: but you belong to Christ and Christ belongs to God" (I Corinthians 3:23).

On the other hand, perhaps we are poorer for not building great churches, great religious monuments. Man puts into architecture what he treasures. He makes visible where his heart is. "For wherever your treasure is, you may be certain that your heart will be there too" (Matthew 6:18). Chesterton expressed it this way. "God does not like cathedrals but he loves cathedral builders." Something seems to happen in the process to the human spirit. We expand to the dimensions of what we built. Our physical architecture creates the horizons of our spirit, gives frontiers to our souls. There are certain cities which expand and reveal the human spirit; other cities oppress and contract.

Rome exercises a universal attraction over the human spirit because it is so totally a City of God and a city of man. She invites all to meet man through the ages and Christ in the ages. Her history embraces all the grandeur and foolishness of humanity. The ancient story is still alive. All the faces of history linger here. Three thousand years continue to breathe their story. Though anchored in the past she is free to move in the present and to create a new future. Rome is a universal city and welcomes everyone home as belonging to her. Anyone reared in the Christian and Western civilization is entitled to call himself a "citizen of Rome," "civis Romanus sum." Christ had been a Roman citizen. St. Paul valued the fact that he was a Roman citizen. When questioned by the tribune in Jerusalem, "Tell me, are you a Roman citizen?" "I am," Paul said. . ."I was born to it" (Acts 22:28). Peter and Paul gravitated to Rome in the power of the command of Christ to make disciples of all nations. The roads to all nations lead through Rome; there they begin and end. "O Blessed Rome that has been consecrated by the blood of the princes of the apostles." The Rome of the martyrs and saints of every age! The Holy City yet the unholy city. The eternal city yet the city in time.

The tomb of John XXIII alongside the tomb of Peter.

The great city is something like the connective tissue among the living cells of knowledge, of beauty, of history. Rome renews itself incessantly through change, destruction and the improvements of all the ages. Today Rome's vitality is undiminished and contains without confusion the still-living ruins of every age known to history. No other city brings into harmony as effortlessly things which would be incongruous elsewhere. Such is the complicated wealth of the city that you are always surprised but never shocked by its infinite medley, the great power of which seems to be an incredible capacity to absorb not only every foreign or exotic importation but even its conquerors.

It has been said that the fountains are the "voice of Rome," at times pleasant and joyful, again melancholy and gloomy. G. K. Chesterton found in the fountains of Rome intimations of resurrection, "I realized that Rome is Rome of the fountains because there is in all of it, this sense of secret things thrust upwards from below. The Tritons might ride aloft as if they were gods of the sky rather than the sea; they might blow their shelly horns tossed up from the deep as if they were the trumpets of the dome; but their exultation was in having dragged up drowned things into the daylight and fished up sunken treasure to glitter in the strong sun of Italy."

Rome has the smell of time, the memory of centuries which live in it. One cannot enter the Catacombs without detecting the scent of leaven, the fermenting seed which was destined to change the world.

Michaelangelo was the originator of the Baroque which has remained since his day the predominant style of Rome. Baroque is a passion for the infinite, a style of inner torment, of desire to reach the unreachable.

Rome is the phoenix of history; reduced again and again by the fury and flames of war to nothing more than a village or modest town. She has always been able, by drawing on the inexhaustible springs of her spirit, to recover her former grand proportions. "Rome rises over each culture but used each one to build upon." St. Clement. Our own Edgar Allen Poe wrote of Rome,

At length, at length, after so many days
of weary pilgrimage and burning thirst
(Thirst for the springs of lore that in thee lie)
I kneel, an altered and humble man,
Amid thy shadows, and so drink within
My very soul thy grandeur, gloom, and glory.

Among the comforts of Rome there is the fact of being the most communal city of the world, where the oddness and difference of nations is little remarked because she happens to be from nature a city pieced together with foreigners and everyone feels at home.

Where can a man learn more knowledge

than in Rome? Everyone comes to Rome and thinks he has found his country. What Rome does best of all is to absorb. It takes to itself people from every part of the world. The real common denominator of this medley of races and dialects is to be found in their familiarity with great and sacred things.

The history of Rome has not ended. If you go there you will find a living city with a future. Rome's significance is still to be found in its insistence on the unity of mankind, on the pre-eminence of the spiritual, on peace and justice through love and compassion, and on order and hierarchy. Rome continues as the heart of our common world and one of the most inspiring words of our civilization.

These were the stream of thoughts and memories which drifted through my mind and heart as I kept the long vigil at the foot of St. Peter's tomb awaiting the opening of the Holy Year Door. It has been twenty years since I studied here within the shadow of St. Peter's. I had lived out another quarter of my life, but Rome had hardly moved a day. I had grown older than Rome, but yet could come back and pick up with her as with an old friend.

Rome is a gentle city. It has a quieting and settling effect upon a person. She touches one with her wisdom, her capacity to survive, her trust in man which is the future. Rome bathes one in such immensity of history and time that one is humbled like Job.

> "I knew you then only by hearsay; but now, having seen you with my own eyes I retract all I have said, and in dust and ashes I repent" (Job 42:5).

Rome is the Church and the Church is humanity. Mother-Church, what incredible paradoxes and contradictions she embraces: all the grandeur and foolishness of men! The strange blend of all that is ancient and all that is not yet; the oldest traditions and the newest freedoms. Because she is anchored in the past she is more free to move in the present. Rome is a mantle of the Church, a Verbum, a Word which has become flesh. She is an invitation to faith, to meet the wounded Christ present in all the ages of humankind. Rome is the still point of pilgrimage because it is the city of saints. No city has been blessed with more saints in every epoch of man. No city has been more of a scandal, from whom so much was expected and so little given. "But however great the number of sins committed, grace was even greater" (Romans 5:21).

"Christ loved the Church and sacrificed himself for her to make her holy. He made her clean by washing her in water with a form of words, so that when he took her to himself she would be glorious, with no speck or wrinkle or anything like that, but holy and faultless" (Ephesians 5:26). Christ takes to himself the Church in every moment of time. Through him the world and all of history is being saved and freed. The Lamb of God is always taking away the sins of the world, of the city, of each of us. Rome is the mirror of humanity in all its history, and there in the heart of all human history and pilgrimage is the Church, the leaven of life, which bears a light that shines in the dark, a "light that darkness could not overpower" (John 1:4). "And the gates of hell shall not prevail against you" (Matthew 16:18).

XII CELTIC MEDITATIONS

"Pray continually and never lose heart" (Luke *18*:1).

"Stay awake, praying at all times" (Luke *21*:36).

"Pray constantly: and for all things give thanks to God" (1 Thessalonians *5*:17).

"So that always and everywhere you are giving thanks to God" (Ephesians *5*:20).

"Always be thankful (eucharistic)" (Colossians *3*:15).

"Never say or do anything except in the name of the Lord Jesus, giving thanks to God the Father through him" (Colossians *3*:17).

"Whatever you eat, whatever you drink, whatever you do at all, do it for the glory of God" (1 Corinthians *10*:31).

"In him, we live and move and have our being" (Acts *17*:28).

"The mysteries of the kingdom of heaven are revealed to you. . .like a treasure hidden in a field. . .a net cast into the sea" (Matthew *13*).

"You must know, the kingdom of God is within you" (Luke *17*:21).

"Unless you change and become like little children, you will never enter the kingdom of heaven" (Matthew *18*:3).

We rarely think of the ordinary actions of everyday—walking, sitting, traveling, sleeping, as prayer. Yet throughout the New Testament we are called to pray always, to enter into the presence of him who is with us in the dailyness of our every day. We are invited to be creative and receptive like little children, and by conscious experience to know, to rejoice in the kingdom of heaven existing within us, around us. "Well, I tell you: Look around you, look at the fields; already they are white, ready for harvest!" (John *4*:35). These are exercises in consciousness, preludes to prayer, practices of the presence of God, invitations to enter into the mind and heart, imagination and emotions of Jesus who shares, lives all our experiences with us. "I am with you always."

TRAVELING

In traveling, new roads, new skies open to expand the mind and heart. One experiences a new freedom and freshness; something is reborn in one. We all delight in travel; few are immune to the wanderlust deep within. As Americans we are highly mobile and seem to be more comfortable in motion than at rest. We probably spend more time on wheels each day than we do at table. When there is nothing to do, many go out just for the drive, just to be in motion. Each year, with our new found leisure, we do more and more traveling. Perhaps a spirituality of traveling will emerge or perhaps we will rediscover the ancient sense of pilgrimage which looks upon every road, every way as a holy one.

Traveling may not be recognized as a spiritual exercise, but it certainly can exercise, stretch the spirit! The world is a sacrament of God, the earth is the face of God. "All things are yours." Until recently, I had limited his country, the Holy Land, to Israel. But I have come more recently to recognize our country as his, all of it holy through his incarnation, redemption, all of it continued in holiness through each one of us. The rivers, plains, the mountains, canyons, the desert, the ocean were made for me, create a new song, new prayer, new psalms in me in the awe, the wonder of gratitude and beauty. It is I who am traveled in and what I discover is what is within me. "And God saw that it was good"—the prayer of Genesis becomes mine in a new deeply rooted way. All of this was made for me, all of it waiting to be seen, to be appreciated, to be delighted in as only I could delight in it. All of this sings its unique song in me. God speaks to me on the way. He journeys in me; the interstate highways become a prayer. He stretches, draws me to his dimensions, giving me new eyes, new ears, a new tongue. "How infinitely great is the power that he has exercised for us believers." "The fullness of him who fills the whole creation." Before the Grand Canyon, one is awesomely conscious that "a thousand years are as one day, and one day is as a thousand years." "God! you are my Grand Canyon, my Rocky Mountains. Your word is a Grand Canyon which can be explored, wondered at endlessly, infinitely. By becoming man, you have made all of this yours; by your Ascension, you have lifted, drawn all things with you, consecrating everything with your love, asking us to continue to consecrate it in remembrance of you. God, you are my ocean; there is so little of you that I can see, so little that I can drink, that I can take into myself."

"Now he is going before you to Galilee: it is there that you will see him." He goes before us; he goes with us in all of our journeyings. He has given us many parables of travelers: the Prodigal Son, the Jericho man, the narrow gate, the road which is wide and spacious. Take nothing for the journey other than a basket for bread, a cup for wine. "I am the Way" (John 6:1).

SITTING

"He sat down (rested) on the seventh day after all the work he had been doing. God blessed the seventh day and made it holy, because on that day he had sat down after all his work of creating" (Genesis 2,2).

"When all is made new and the Son of Man sits on his throne of glory, you will yourselves sit on twelve thrones" (Matthew *19*,28).

"He ascended into heaven and sits at the right hand of the Father." Creed. "living forever to intercede for all who come to God through him" (Hebrews *7*,25).

"Seeing the crowds, he went up the hill. There he sat down and was joined by his disciples" (Matthew *5*,1).

"He then rolled up the scroll, gave it back to the assistant and sat down. And all eyes in the synagogue were fixed on him. Then he began to speak to them" (Luke *4*,19).

"Get them to sit down" (Luke *9*,14). Miracle of the loaves.

"So he sat down...He then took a little child, set him in front of them, put his arms round him, and said to them..." (Mark *9*,35).

"When evening came he was at table with the twelve disciples...Now as they were eating, Jesus took some bread..." (Matthew *26*,20).

Sitting is the posture of rest, of receptivity, of listening, of refreshment, of eating, of learning, of reading, of writing. Sitting is the posture of prayer, of Eucharist, of celebrating, feasting, of family and friendship.

How good it is to sit down when the work is done and time is not hanging over you.

How many the places, how many the ways in which we sit: sitting at work, at table, before the window, around the altar, alongside the hearth, at a bedside; to sit on a hill, upon the earth, under the shade of a tree. "I saw you under the fig tree" (John 2,48). Matthew was sitting by the customs house. The two blind men were sitting by the side of the road when Jesus passed by. Jesus was sitting at table when his feet were washed by Magdalene's tears and again when they were anointed for his burial. The apostles were sitting when Jesus washed their feet.

How renewing it is to sit in one's favorite chair, in the warmth of an old rocker, to sit and rock to the tune and rhythm of one's own heart, to rest, to think, to be, perhaps to dream, experiencing the quiet joy of being alive, healthy, graced, friended—the old Sunday afternoon feeling. It may be experiencing the transcendental quiet which comes in listening to music.

The Buddhists have a whole school of sitting meditation called "Zazen."

Much of our sitting is done in the car behind the driving wheel, in our mobile hermitage and cloister. This affords great privacy and seclusion for many people, alone on the crowded freeway. Once the mechanical concentration of driving is mastered, the inner spirit is free to reflect, to think, listen, pray, We seldom speak to our unknown companions on the road, our pilgrim fellow travelers, each on their own quest. We are each on our way into Jerusalem, sitting, not on a donkey, but on wheels. He sits up front with us. He is our constant companion, the one who breaks bread with us, the one who has promised, "I will never leave you alone" (John *14*,18).

SLEEPING

"So Yahweh God made man fall into a deep sleep" (Genesis *3*,21).

"He gives sleep to those he loves" (Psalms *127*,2).

"Now I can lie down and go to sleep and then awake, for Yahweh has hold of me" (Psalms *3*,5).

"In peace I lie down, and fall asleep at once, since you alone, Yahweh, make me rest secure" (Psalms *4*,8).

"The boat was almost swamped. But he was in the stern, his head on a cushion, asleep" (Mark *4*,38).

"Peter and his companions were heavy with sleep, but they kept awake and saw his glory" (Luke *9*,32).

"He came back a third time and said to them, 'You can sleep on now and take your rest. It is all over' " (Mark *14*,41).

God does not like men who do not sleep at night. Sleep is one of God's most beautiful gifts to men. Sleep is the friend of man. Sleep is the friend of God. Peguy.

The joy of going to bed at night! The bed of conception, of birth, of suffering, of love, of death. The consolation of deep sleep. The sleep of ordinary tiredness, the sleep of exhaustion. The world of the dream, and the unconscious. The great epic dreams I have had, the dreams of a child. The remembrance of things past, of roads traveled, people loved. The memory banks, treasuring the echoes of my entire life. Waking up at night and falling back to sleep. Awake in one's own dream.

The last moments of the day before falling asleep and the first moments of awakening from sleep are privileged times for prayer. The first, the last moments of sleep are sacramentals, holy moments, special times of consciousness. It is then that we are closest to the depths, the ground of our being.

Sleep is the time to rest with abundant peace and love in the heart of my God who watches and slumbers not. Blessed are you who sleep in the Lord. While I sleep he keeps the city. In the night of my sleep, he turns all of the earth upon her axis and fashions from darkness a new day of light. Sleep surrounds the heart of man with solitude. Sleep is the secret of being tireless.

In the night of sleep, man dreams and the Lord his God calls. Jacob dreamed the ladder. Samuel heard the voice. A word was brought to Job. He caught a whisper of it during the vision of night when deep sleep fell upon him. (Job *4*).

A messenger of God appeared to Joseph in sleep over and again. "Get up, take the child and his mother with you" (Matthew *2*,13).

"I sleep, yet my heart is awake" (Canticle *5*,2).

Then waking up to the joy, the excitement of a new day, a day which the Lord had made; in awe and wonder at a day yet to be breathed, filled with his Spirit.

> "I say this prayer to you, Yahweh,
>   for at daybreak you listen for my voice;
>   and at dawn I hold myself in readiness
>   for you,
>   I watch for you" (Psalms *5*,3).

WALKING

> "the sound of Yahweh God walking in the garden in the cool of the day" (Genesis *3*:8).

> "walk before me and be perfect" (Genesis *17*:1).

> "As he was walking by the sea. . .he said to them, follow me" (Matthew *4*:20).

> "he came toward them, walking on the lake."

> "follow in my footsteps" (Matthew *10*:39).

> "Walk while you have the light" (John *12*:35).

> "Walk in love as Christ loved us" (Ephesians *5*:2).

"Walk worthy of your vocation" (Ephesians
4:1).

"Now as they talked this over, Jesus himself
came up and walked by their side" (Luke
24:15).

God walked and talked with Adam and
Eve in the cool of the evening. Jesus
walked with his disciples the length and
breadth of Galilee, Samaria, Judea. He
walked the lake, the hills, the mountains
and the plains, Mt. Hermon, Mt. Tabor, the
Mount of Olives. He walked the streets of
the towns and villages. Every walk of ours
is an Emmaus Walk, he walks by our side,
even though there is "something preventing
us from recognizing him."

Walking is a kind of seeing, a kind of
feeling, a kind of being present, rendering
oneself present. There is a school of philosophy, the peripatetic followers of Aristotle,
who developed their philosophy by walking
up and down, back and forth, the body
turning the mind over every facet of the
subject. There is a school of meditation in
Zen Buddhism which does its meditation
through walking.

There is a way of knowing a place
because you have put it under foot. You
come on a place because you have foot-
printed it as carefully as if you had passed
it through your hands. Grass and asphalt,
wood and concrete, rock and sand give
distinctive pressures to each foot fall. Walk-

ing brings with it a gentleness, a calmness, an openness, a freedom. Weather brings a newness to each walk—rain walks, sun walks, wind walks, snow walks. And the sounds and echoes of walking! It is in walking that one discovers the moods and music, the voices and silences of the city and woods, the river and lake.

The most natural form of movement is the human step, man's pace—three miles an hour, thirty a day! How long it took to learn the rhythm of lifting our legs, swinging our arms! Each person has his own unique stride, her own personal rhythm. The whole body responds. The arms dance to the feet, the breath fills the chest, becomes deeper and fuller. Each person treads the earth distinctively, on heel or ball, or both together.

We walk for the sheer joy of walking, to stretch ourselves to our fullest dimensions. We walk on top of the earth or on the bottom like a fly on the ceiling held by gravity alone. The earth holds us to herself with the gravity of love.

I wonder how mother earth responds to the touch of all of our feet: Barefoot and sandals, boots and slippers, work shoes and play shoes, the heaviness and gentleness of feet! The first step of the child and the last step of the dying man; the Springtime of walking and the Autumn of walking; the Calvary walk, the Ascension walk. All walking is a blessing, a prayer. Walk in the newness of life. Walk in faith and in the spirit. Watch and listen for his footsteps.

POSTSCRIPT COMMEMORATION
A SACRED PLACE

Sacred Heart Seminary
1924—1974

"Truly, the Lord is in this place and I never
knew it. . .How awe-inspiring this place is!
This is nothing less than a house of God; this
is the gate of heaven! (Genesis 28:16)

July 26, 1701—founding of Detroit—
March 8, 1833. Establishment of the
Diocese—September 22, 1924. Opening of
Sacred Heart Seminary on Chicago
Boulevard.

What is in a name? What makes a place
significant? It is people who make a place
significant, why they come together, what
happens to them there, what spirit is
enkindled and continued there.

Where God meets men in a special way,
that place becomes holy. "Take off your
shoes, for the place on which you stand is
holy ground" (Exodus 3:5).

This seminary is a holy place because of
those whom he has called here to be
initiated into discipleship and ministry.
This is hallowed ground, these are hallowed
walls because of the cumulative presence of
the prayer, penance, study, discipline,
laughter and tears of 1111 priests who have

lived here. Their years in this place are imbedded forever.

A seminary is a special environment, a faith community of men who like the first disciples are asking the question "Where do you live?" and who hear him say "Come and see" (John *1*:39). A seminary is a fraternity of men who believe his promise, "Follow me and I will make you into fishers of men" (Mark *1*:18)—"and at once they left their nets and followed him."

Each seminarian makes visible the echo of Christ's words: "If anyone wants to be a follower of mine, let him renounce himself and take up his cross every day and follow me. For anyone who wants to save his life will lose it; but anyone who loses his life for my sake, that man will save it" (Luke *9*:23).

A seminary is indeed a place to die, for it is a place of Resurrection. Where the seed goes into the ground and dies, new life will emerge.

A seminary is a gathering-together-place for ordinary men led by an extraordinary Spirit.

Sacred Heart Seminary is the Nazareth of today thrust into the center of a contemporary Jerusalem. This is a place of solitude, a place of community, a place of rest, a place of most intense activity; a place and a time to search, to test, to explore, to discover—the contemporary Christ, the contemporary man and woman, the contemporary world and city, the contemporary priest.

A diocese is a place; it is a people. A diocesan priest is a man committed to a place, to a people. For him there is a special permanence of place, of time, a deep-rootedness, an anchored stability in ever moving waters, a built-in Gibraltar-ness which stands between oceans ever changing and breaking.

The presence of this seminary, its very structure, is a call, an invitation, a challenge. The cumulative spirit and life deposited here by so many over the years creates a field of force, an energy field across this city and diocese which is ever drawing, compelling, in season and out of season, during lean years and prosperous years.

This place is a center of prayer and dedication, an undiminishing radioactivity of grace which emits rays of faith, hope and love far beyond what eye can see, ear hear, or hand touch.

At full tide or low tide, it still stands through the night, a monument of the living faith of a diocese which has no intention of fading or dying.

The heart, the womb of a diocese is its seminary, the holder, the preserver of its wisdom and tradition, the hope and guarantee of its future.

The men of Sacred Heart Seminary "look to the past with reverence, to the present with responsibility, and to the future with faith, which is the substance of hope."

They dare to sing out "You see this city, this seminary? Here God lives among men. He will make his home among them; they shall be his people, and he will be their God; his name is God-with-them" (Revelations 21:3).